THE MILITARY REVOL
AND THE STATE
1500-1800

Edited by Michael Duffy

EXETER STUDIES IN HISTORY   No. 1

Published by the University of Exeter 1980

First published 1980 by the University of Exeter
Second impression 1981
Third impression 1986

EXETER STUDIES IN HISTORY

General Editor: Colin Jones

Editorial Committee

Mrs B.J. Coles, BA MPhil FSA
M.D.D. Newitt, BA PhD FRHistS
M. Duffy, MA DPhil
Professor I.A. Roots, MA FSa FRHistS

Publications

Exeter University Publications,
Hailey Wing,
Reed Hall,
Streatham Drive,
Exeter EX4 4QR

ISBN 0 85989 111 9
ISSN 0260 8628

Printed and Bound by A. Wheaton & Co. Ltd., Exeter

CONTENTS

Acknowledgements

The authors wish to thank Judith Saywell, Hilary Tolley, Janet Stiling, Seán Goddard and Stephen Roberts without whose obliging and tolerant assistance this volume could not have been produced. The Editor also gratefully acknowledges the unflagging efforts of Colin Jones in getting the series launched.

Introduction: The Military Revolution and the State 1500-1800

MICHAEL DUFFY

In 1956 Michael Roberts expounded the concept of a 'Military Revolution' between the years 1560 and 1660 which 'exercised a profound influence upon the future course of European history' and stood 'like a great divide separating medieval society from the modern world'.[1] Subsequent commentators, most notably Geoffrey Parker, while criticizing Roberts's explanation of this revolution and extending its dates from 1530 to 1710, have nevertheless accepted the general thesis.[2] In the sixteenth and seventeenth centuries there was an enormous growth in the size of the permanent armed forces of European states as well as in the numbers they mobilized for war.[3] By the late seventeenth century these forces were better disciplined than ever before and much more uniform within each state in weapons, drill and dress. They were paid and maintained by the state on a professional basis to a far greater extent, and to accommodate and sustain these developments there was a major growth in state bureaucracy, state finance and state intervention in the economy and society. The net result was a great increase in the power of the state in early modern Europe. The following articles seek to explain these developments in the cases of the main exemplars of land power (France) and naval power (Britain) and also to show the consequences for a state (Portugal) which faced similar problems but failed to press through the full extent of the Military Revolution.

The precise reasons for the expansion in size of European armies and navies are still matter for debate. Parker and Michael Howard have stressed the evolution of the bastioned-trace which so much strengthened fortification in land warfare that both a larger besieging army was required to attack the fortification and at the same time a large covering army was necessary to guard against attempts at relief in sieges which inevitably lasted longer.[4] The Age of Discovery called for an increase in both land and sea forces to take advantage of the new overseas opportunities. The impact and example of the large Ottoman armies and fleets which began to penetrate Central Europe and the Mediterranean in the sixteenth century cannot be ignored. Finally the logic of an increase in numbers once there was a reversion to linear tactics to accommodate the new strength of fire power must be stressed. On land, lines had to be strengthened by the addition of second or third lines in reserve to prevent penetration and lengthened to prevent

them being outflanked and rolled up. At sea, the addition of second
or third tiers of guns to warships strengthened the line and extra ships
extended it to prevent it being 'doubled' by an enemy. In practice,
once an arms race had started each state needed to expand its armed
forces to prevent a rival gaining the advantage in battle or siege. The
only limits imposed were those of command structure in an age of bad
communications and of the availability of finance, supplies and manpower adequate to sustain expanding forces. If these barriers could
be broken then the Military Revolution could be extended until such
limitations reimposed themselves again at a larger size.

The stages by which these limitations were broken and the points
at which they reappeared as restraints are considered below.[5] The
organisation of the initial stage of expansion was largely beyond the
resources of the fifteenth and sixteenth-century state in terms of recruitment and pay. Some states, like Portugal, tried to revive and
expand a semi-feudalistic system of recruitment through the nobles
who collected retainers and paid them from plunder. This method was
not without remarkable initial success, but limitations soon re-emerged.
All states then turned to the military entrepreneur - the private-
enterprise military organiser who raised troops on contract and
supported himself and his men partly through state pay but more through
plunder and forced contributions.[6] At this stage the entrepreneur
provided the lower-level military organisation which the state lacked,
and during the Thirty Years' War Wallenstein even supplied at all levels
a complete military organisation with its own armaments and supply
back-up. A better financed variant of this system was the corporate
overseas trading company developed by the states of the North-
Western European seaboard. These were armed organisations extending state power and their own profit through gun-boat trading diplomacy
and at times their trading side was merely a respectable front for
ruthless semi-piratical fighting bodies drawing profits from plunder.
The Dutch West India Company was the prime example of the corporate
commercial military entrepreneur but the Dutch and British East India
Companies were not far removed from it.

Quite apart from the danger of a Cromwell or a Wallenstein
becoming too powerful, the problem of the entrepreneurial system was
that plunder was not unlimited nor without devastating economic effects
and eventually threatened to quench the fount of wealth and sustenance.
Over-reliance on plunder and exploitation brought Portuguese state
expansion to a full stop. Other states managed to limit plunder or
harness it to state ends in a less destructive fashion so as to keep
their newly expanded forces in being in a new form, directly controlled,
recruited, organised and paid by the state itself.

The necessity for this transition into the final stage of the Military
Revolution and the mode by which it was accomplished are examined in
the study of the French army. At sea, where the private enterprise

fighter did less damage to primary production of wealth and where he
was less politically dangerous, the entrepreneurial system was allowed
to continue in the form of state-licensed privateers whose operations
supplemented those of the expanded, professional, state-controlled
navy. However, the enormous cost of sea-warfare in specialized ships
and dockyard facilities meant that privateers were small-scale organisations compared with the military entrepreneur of former years.
Only the state could afford to build and maintain the largest warships,
just as on land only the state could afford to build and maintain the
great fortresses and extensive fortifications around towns which now
dominated land warfare. Once the state discovered the financial means
to exploit and elaborate the new military developments to the full it
moved into expenditure well beyond the reach of the private entrepreneur. The Military Revolution must be measured not only in terms of
manpower expansion (which the entrepreneur could initially supply but
ultimately not maintain) but also in terms of numbers of ever larger
ships and modern fortresses with all the necessary logistical back-up
to build and maintain them. These the entrepreneur could not produce
except outside Europe where, because of the difficulties in assembling
the logistical back-up for European-style warfare, ship and fortress
size did not need to be so large and so the trading companies could
keep up with state resources for a century more. Throughout Europe
however the state was forced to develop its own organisation, particularly a money-collecting machinery which could meet these extended
requirements of modern warfare, and so moved beyond reliance on the
entrepreneur.

The effects of the Military Revolution were felt in almost every
aspect of European life. The creation of such vast state-organised
armed forces was perhaps the most considerable achievement of the
Ancien Régime, matched only by its success in subordinating them to
civilian control. André Corvisier has suggested that in the period
1560-1660 proportionately more Europeans were under arms than at
any period before modern times.[7] Matters had threatened to get out
of hand. Not only did the military entrepreneurs spread their recruiting nets all over Europe, but the civilian population also took up
arms to fight for or against the state, to resist the plundering of
entrepreneurial armies, and to protect themselves against the widespread brigandage of this anarchic period, so that the distinction
between civilian and soldier almost disappeared. Through the Military
Revolution the entrepreneurs were brought under control and eventually
eliminated by the professional, disciplined standing army of the state.
A clear distinction between soldiers and civilians was re-established.
The civilian no longer needed to train himself to arms, and everywhere
in Europe the old militia system of the citizen soldier fell into decline.
In Spain in 1692, where 495,000 men were on the militia rolls, only
59,000 (12.7%) were actually armed.[8] Even in France enrolment in
the militia was basically inclusion in a reserve list enabling the wartime expansion of the army; regular training was minimal. Instead

of the civilian having to defend himself the standing army did it for
him, acting in both an internal policing role and as defence against
foreign foes.

The subordination of soldiers to civilian control and their large-
scale establishment as a separate and permanent entity within the
state, as well as the construction of large navies and great modern
fortresses, involved an enormous advance in state administration and
a growing involvement of the state in the day-to-day lives of its
subjects. Many aspects of this can be traced in the articles on France
and Britain. The new large standing armies alone brought more
people into state service than ever before. In a small state such as
Sweden or Prussia, struggling to maintain an army commensurate with
other great Powers, this could bring as many as 1 in 13 or 14 of the
population directly under state control as soldiers,[9] and large numbers
more were involved in equipping, feeding and administering them.
New methods of taxation and of loan finance had to be devised and
administered by the state to pay for the expanded armed forces. Their
recruitment, equipment and maintenance all had to be organised by
state officials. Indeed for all the glittering facade of a Versailles or
a Sans Souci the governments of Ancien Régime Europe were really
giant war-making machines devoting their main efforts to the maintenance of large armed forces.[10] The principal elements of the state
bureaucracies that now developed were a Treasury to finance armies
and navies and a War Ministry and Navy or Admiralty Department to
administer them.

This same strengthening and extending of the administration also
had an obvious effect on the restoration of political stability and the
enforcement of law and order after the 'general crisis of the seventeenth century'. The monarchs and governments of Europe now had
large, disciplined armed forces which enabled them to maintain order,
and which, together with their associated bureaucracies, were also a
substantial source of job-opportunities. Louis XIV did not control his
nobility by keeping them idle at Versailles but by providing state
employments for them. Impoverished and discontented nobles could
become officers, others along with the ambitious bourgeoisie could
join the bureaucracy, while in the ranks 'sturdy beggars', paupers and
vagrants would find food and clothing. In a way it was a system of
state welfare effectively bringing under control the unemployed and
discontented. Corvisier has calculated that in the armed forces alone
in France, if serving officers, old officers, gentlemen serving as
soldiers (usually in élite cavalry or guards regiments) and naval
officers are taken together, then there were some 20-25,000 jobs held
by gentilshommes in 1775.[11] The substantial part this played in
controlling the turbulent French nobility can be seen in the disaffection
not only of nobles but also of disappointed bourgeois aspirants when
prior to the French Revolution the War Minister Saint-Germain cut
back the ranks of the officer corps.

Besides providing state employment, the Military Revolution
led the state into extending its control over other civilian employments.
In Prussia the main tax-collecting agency was called, significantly,
the General War Commissariat, and its task of supplying the necessary back-up to the Prussian army led it into the supervision of
police and of municipal administration (through its collection of the
excise tax levied on towns), into the promotion of commerce, industry
and immigration, and (probably because most cities were walled and
might be liable to siege) into the control of city planning and development and public works construction. [12] Concern to sustain the Military
Revolution also led the state to intervene more directly in education.
Whereas before, education had largely been left to the church and to
local bodies with the state only supplying endowments and occasional
subsidies, now the state intervened more directly in certain aspects
to provide finance, teachers, and to shape the syllabus. It has been
claimed that the most significant educational development in Germany
in the seventeenth and early eighteenth centuries was the creation of
Ritterakademien at which the nobility were given an education to enable
them to act as officers in the army. [13] In Eastern Europe this initiated
the first steps at compulsory state education both in Prussia and in
Russia where Peter the Great decreed in 1717 that all sons of the
nobility should attend either the Naval Academy, the Engineering
Academy or the Artillery Academy at St. Petersburg. Between 1714
and 1716 the Tsar also issued decrees for the sons of bourgeois and
of non-noble government officials to receive a compulsory education
in figures and geometry administered by the Admiralty. [14] Even in
Britain the first educational establishment of a modern kind, directly
and fully financed on a regular basis by the state and with its staff
appointed and syllabus directed by the state, was the Naval Academy
established at Portsmouth in 1729.

The Military Revolution equally led to a greater state intervention in medicine. For example the 'enormous advance' in medicine
and medical education in Prussia between 1713 and 1725 has been
ascribed jointly to Frederick William I's intense interest in the Prussian
army and to his paternalistic concern for the welfare of his subjects.
In 1713 the Anatomical Theatre was founded at Berlin to train surgeons
for the army. In 1723 the College of Medicine and Surgery was established and in the following year the King ordered that all surgeon-
candidates in Prussia must attend its lectures on anatomy and operating procedure and after qualification they would be obliged to serve
for a time as regimental field-surgeons. [15]

To supply the expanded armed forces involved considerable
state intervention in the economy, as the article on the British navy
indicates. The state became the biggest single purchaser of food,
clothing and metalware and the biggest shipbuilder in maritime areas;
it became the biggest single source of employment for the construction
industry in its demand for dockyards, for barracks and for

fortifications - particularly this latter since the entire system of fortification of all towns and strongpoints in Europe had to be modernized to the bastioned-trace system. The effect of this great new source of demand and expenditure on the European economy has yet to be fully estimated.[16] In some states military demand was the very basis of industrial development. In Russia it was responsible for the beginnings of the iron and textile industries, of the sailcloth and rope making industries and a great stimulus to the lumber industry.[17] In some states the Military Revolution was even used to provide manpower for industrial development. In the textile industry production of spun yarn often lagged behind weaving so that Prussian soldiers were encouraged to take up spinning in their barracks in off-duty hours, while in Austria in 1768 soldiers and their dependents were actually ordered to employ themselves in linen, woollen and cotton spinning when they were not on military duty in order to assist local industry.[18]

Doubtless the Military Revolution diverted the European economy into artificial paths, but such paths led to employment and profit. Doubtless taxation to pay for the armed forces was regressive, but the money was immediately put back into the economy. Through state taxation and borrowing there was a significant redistribution of capital in the economy either directly into industry and agriculture through purchases of equipment and supplies or indirectly through the buying power of soldiers and sailors who were never conspicuous savers. It has yet to be proven that money mobilised and redeployed within the economy in this way would have been otherwise invested in such a wide variety of economic pursuits. It may be that if the states of Europe had not fought each other their economies would have advanced quicker, though this is debatable - in addition to points already made, other spin-offs such as the evolution of credit finance and insurance institutions and the development of managerial techniques might be noted.[19] In any case to think that states would or could have so restrained themselves from war in the absence of any powerful and obvious deterrent is to fly in the face of history. Of course there were advantages in neutrality, but neutrality was a luxury only available to those on the fringe of the main battle-zones (such as the United States or the Baltic States in the late eighteenth century). At all times the continuance of such neutrality was at the whim of the warring powers - witness the relations of those particular neutrals with Britain. Britain itself was not allowed the neutrality it wished in 1688. Holland's attempts to get out of the arms-race failed miserably in the second half of the eighteenth century. The fact was that governments which did not participate in the Military Revolution were likely to be plundered and have their economy destroyed by more powerful states. Britain and France were amongst the principal despoilers. Portugal and Poland, which failed to participate in the full extent of the Military Revolution in time, and Spain and Holland which were unable to sustain it, were amongst the principal despoiled. While it is possible that participation in the Military Revolution was an internal economic handicap, at least those

who kept up with it were saved from total economic disaster at the
hands of rival plundering Powers seeking trade monopolies and other
economic or military advantages.

If the economic effects of the Military Revolution are debatable,
its effect on the governments of the Ancien Régime is more certain,
for the expanded armies and navies eventually helped to destroy the
governments that had brought them into being. Like Frankenstein's
monster they developed a momentum of their own and an influence on
the state which governments were powerless to restrain if they were
to continue the international power-struggle. Instead of an army or
navy being a weapon to be used in an independent foreign policy,
foreign policy had to become geared to the requirements of maintaining
a strong army or navy - of gaining new manpower or financial resources;
of ensuring a regular supply of ship-building and other war materials;
and of depriving a potential enemy of these same resources. The
immense costs of the new war-machine brought a new limitation
between about 1695 and 1715 when further expansion of the forces of
existing great Powers was halted and a degree of retrenchment
introduced. The ability to meet such costs proved a far more effective dividing line between great or small Powers than had ever existed
in the previous age of smaller armies and navies. Only a state such
as Prussia which ruthlessly subordinated the whole country to the needs
of the army and at the same time was very careful to husband its
resources by not risking its forces too much in war could now rise
from the small into the ranks of the great Powers. The general trend
was in the other direction. Sheer cost forced Sweden, Holland and
Spain downward. Even the surviving great Powers eventually ran into
difficulties. In 1788 26.3% of French state expenditure went to maintain its armed forces and 49.3% into servicing debts incurred in using
these forces in previous wars - a burden which French government
finances were decreasingly able to meet.[20] The government sought
new sources of taxation, creating new discontent. By economizing too
on military pay, perquisites and offices it alienated the armed forces
which might have enabled it to resist discontent and force through its
proposed reforms. The result was the eventual collapse of government
in the Revolution. The demand of Britain that its American colonies
take on a greater share of military costs had already produced trans-
atlantic revolution, and the attempt to keep costs down by steadfastly
refusing to increase naval pay led to the great mutinies of 1797. It
was the cost of warfare and the expense of maintaining such large
armed forces that was the main impetus towards government attempts
at reform in the second half of the eighteenth century. This in turn
precipitated popular reaction in the Age of Revolutions after 1763.
Armed forces and state power - in both its internal and external facets -
were inseparably connected in early modern Europe. These articles
should contribute towards an elucidation of these relationships.

8

NOTES

. M. Roberts, The Military Revolution, 1560-1660. An Inaugural
Lecture delivered before Queen's University of Belfast (Belfast
1956), reprinted in M. Roberts Essays in Swedish History (London
1967). The quotations are from page 195 of the latter.

2. G. Parker, 'The "Military Revolution" - a myth?', Journal of
Modern History Vol. XLVIII (1976) pp.195-214. See also
M. Howard, War in European History (Oxford 1976), pp.20-74.

3. In addition to British and French examples given below, there is
an estimate of the growth of European armies in The New
Cambridge Modern History, Vol. XIII (Cambridge 1979), in the
chapter on 'Warfare' by G. Parker (p.205) elaborating on his
J.M.H. article (p.206). There is a fuller survey of the size of
eighteenth-century armies in A. Corvisier, Armées et sociétés
en Europe de 1494 à 1789 (Paris 1976), p.126.

4. Howard op.cit. pp.35-36; Parker J.M.H. XLVIII p.208. Parker
also suggests that the change of emphasis from expensive cavalry
to cheap foot soldiers enabled states to field more men. This may
have helped start the expansion but numbers soon considerably
exceeded in cost the former cavalry-based armies.

5. For additional examination of the logistical problems of the
Military Revolution on land see M. van Creveld, Supplying War.
Logistics from Wallenstein to Patton (Cambridge 1977), Chapter 1.

6. The best study of the entrepreneur is F. Redlich, The German
Military Enterpriser and his work force. A study in European
economic and social history (2 vols., Wiesbaden, 1965).

7. Corvisier op.cit. p.18.

8. Ibid. p.21.

9. Ibid. p.126.

10. A recent survey of the senatorial system of government in Russia
in the eighteenth century concludes that its basic purpose 'never
ceased to be the creation of a domestic administration that could
furnish a steady, predictable quantity of men and supplies for the
purposes of war'. G.L. Yaney, The systemization of Russian
government. Social evolution in the domestic adminstration of
Imperial Russia, 1711-1900 (Chicago 1973), p.51.

11. Corvisier op.cit. p.116. Corvisier estimates the proportion of
army officers alone to nobility as 1/33 in France in 1775
deteriorating to 1/40 in 1789. In Prussia it was 1/7 in 1740 and
1/10 in 1786. Such officers obviously had a vested interest in
maintaining a regime which paid and honoured them.

12. R.A. Dorwart, The Prussian welfare state before 1740,
    (Cambridge, Mass. 1971), p.82 n.20.

13. Ibid. p.148

14. Redlich op.cit. II p.116; I. Grey, Peter the Great, (London 1960),
    p.407; B. Dmytryshyn, Modernisation of Russia under Peter I
    and Catherine II (New York 1974), p.11.

15. Dorwart op.cit. pp.261, 266. For the influence of military
    medicine on civilian practice in Britain see J.M. Winter ed.
    War and economic development. Essays in memory of David
    Joslin (Cambridge 1975), pp.73-90: 'Swords and ploughshares:
    the armed forces, medicine and public health in the late eighteenth
    century' by P. Matthias.

16. Parker suggests that the Military Revolution probably retarded
    the economic development of most participants although it
    stimulated neutrals. See J.M.H. XLVIII p.214 and Parker's
    article 'War and economic change: the economic costs of the
    Dutch Revolt' in War and economic development pp.49-71.
    Other contributions to War and economic development are
    however more equivocal: see Winter's summary of research
    pp.4-7 and Matthias's comments p.73.

17. Grey op.cit. pp.414-5; J. Blum, Lord and Peasant in Russia
    from the Ninth to the Nineteenth Century (New York 1967), p.293.

18. Redlich op.cit. II, p.84.

19. Ibid. p.269-70. Redlich concludes his examination of the impact
    of the Military Revolution on the German economy by stating
    that 'I do not believe that a beneficial influence can be doubted.'
    (p.270).

20. P. Goubert, L'Ancien Régime, Vol. II, Les pouvoirs (Paris 1973),
    p.137.

1. Plunder and the Rewards of Office in the Portuguese Empire

MALYN NEWITT

1. The Origin of the Expansion of Portugal's Armed Forces: the Crown's Trade Monopoly

During the fifteenth century the Portuguese initiated and developed a prosperous trade with the African states of the Congo and Guinea regions. The trade was organised on familiar medieval lines. The crown declared a monopoly and then either traded directly itself or licensed private traders, taking a percentage of the profits. Gradually military and diplomatic pressure forced foreign competitors from the field until by 1479 they had been totally excluded from the whole north-eastern Atlantic region (except for the Canary Islands). The monopoly was operated by setting up factories, again on the medieval model, where trade could be conducted all the year by resident merchants or royal factors, and by embassies to African kings which sought to engage the latters' economic power on the side of Portuguese trading interests. The success of this policy could be seen not only in the extent to which the trade of the trans-Saharan caravans was siphoned off, but also in the way in which exchange between the West African kingdoms themselves was promoted, the Portuguese providing maritime transport which these states had hitherto lacked. In this way new markets were opened for African producers.

This West African commercial empire was clearly within the administrative capabilities of a late-medieval state, although the difficulties of communication over great distances were already beginning to become apparent. However, after the return of Vasco da Gama from his exploratory voyage to India in 1499, serious problems arose concerning the best way to exploit the vast new commercial opportunities that had been opened up. By 1504, after only three more voyages to India, a remarkably bold decision was made, one that still ranks among the most daring assertions of state power. The crown decided to try to monopolise the total trade in spices between Europe and the East. This required a series of agreements with the principal exporting states and the imposition of a naval blockade at the mouths of the Red Sea and Persian Gulf. Within a decade, however, this policy had been extended to an attempt to control all seaborne trade in the Indian Ocean. Apart from simple motives of profit, the reason for this extension of the monopoly was that, in order to purchase spices, the Portuguese needed commodities which could only be obtained in other eastern markets - for instance cloth from Cambay (Gujerat in northern India) or Coromandel, gold and ivory from east Africa, or horses from the Persian Gulf. As Portugal had nothing to export herself, apart from scarce precious metals, she was forced to participate in eastern commerce and thought naturally of trying to monopolise its principal commodities.

To implement this policy, as the Portuguese tried to do throughout the sixteenth century, was a complex commercial and military operation which required a great extension of the powers, the administrative structures and the armed forces of the state. It involved the issuing of licenses to all Asiatic traders in the Indian Ocean requiring them to call at designated Portuguese ports to pay customs dues; declaring certain commodities to be a royal monopoly and establishing a system of royal factories to conduct trade in these items; and maintaining fortresses at strategic positions with armed warships to patrol the coasts and secure compliance with the system. It also involved a complex network of diplomatic missions to obtain the goodwill of mainland potentates or, failing that, to offer them 'protection'.

As developed during the governorships of Francisco de Almeida (1505-1509) and Afonso de Albuquerque (1509-1515) the plan was to garrison strategic fortresses at Ormuz in the Persian Gulf, Malacca, Sofala in the Mozambique channel and Aden. These were supported by a major base at Goa, the principal horse-trading port, and by more or less close alliances with the rajas of Cochin and Cananor, the sultan of Melinde, and the sovereigns of Persia and the Hindu state of Vijayanagar. However, this relatively simple imperial structure was never completed for Aden was not captured. In the years after Albuquerque's death its simplicity was inevitably lost as viceroys tried to plug the gaps in the system. By the middle of the century the Portuguese were actively implicated in Ceylon and Ethiopia, had acquired a major fortress at Diu in Gujerat, another at Muscat and were fast becoming a land power in Western India. By the end of the century the structure of the empire had grown still further. Fifty fortresses were garrisoned and territorial commitments had been taken on in East Africa, Ceylon and Western India.

2. Difficulties of Administering the Monopoly

The Portuguese state was little better equipped than any of its contemporaries to administer such a trade monopoly on a world-wide scale or to keep the strings of military, economic and political affairs of India, Indonesia, Persia and East Africa in its hands. Nevertheless the development of the West African monopoly had given it a certain

limited experience. The royal monopoly there was controlled by the
Casa da Guine, a prototype of a modern Ministry, which handled the
supply of fleets, the purchase and sale of goods and the staffing of the
empire. Three trading factories had been established, staffed by a
paid garrison and by factors who acted as servants of the crown and
received a salary. Here were the rudiments of a professional,
salaried bureaucracy existing to fulfil the commercial objectives of
state policy. It was to be the model taken for the development of the
much larger monopoly in the East. However, during the fifteenth
century the Portuguese had also successfully carried out the coloni-
sation of four groups of islands in the Atlantic and for this purpose a
devolved and quasi-feudal arrangement had been adopted. The islands
had been granted as hereditary 'captaincies' to individual Portuguese
in return for the duty to settle, develop and defend them, the crown
reserving to itself only residual jurisdictions and trading and fiscal
rights.

After the return of Vasco da Gama from India, therefore, the
crown devised a scheme for administering the trade of the East through
a bureaucratic structure of officials and soldiers, all serving its
commercial interests as paid servants. The royal monopolies were
handled by a greatly expanded Casa da Guine, renamed Casa da India.
The spices were sold through a factory established at Antwerp. In
India all Portuguese were employees of the crown, their lives regu-
lated by detailed sets of instructions. All received salaries and
allowances for food, strictly graded according to their rank. Care was
taken to see that the forts and factories had a full complement of
skilled craftsmen and military experts. Regulations covered in detail
the handling of cargoes and even the daily lives of the garrisons to
ensure that relations with local peoples remained good and that the
royal monopolies were not infringed by private trading.

Such a bureaucracy was, in concept, ahead of its time, and it
faced problems in its realisation which made it totally impractical.
First, there was the problem of communication. Although correspon-
dence could be exchanged between West Africa and Lisbon in a matter
of months, it regularly took up to two years for an exchange of letters
with stations in the East. Moreover even in the East communication
was difficult between the isolated factories and the headquarters at
Cochin or, after 1530, at Goa. The seasonal monsoons only made the
problems worse. Here it should be noted how much more favourably
placed were the Castilians who could exchange letters with their
Caribbean empire within three months.

Second, there was from the start an acute shortage of resources.
Although ship-building was expanded and Portugal used considerable
ingenuity in devising new forms of vessel, arms had to be imported
and precious metals had to be purchased on the exchanges of the
Netherlands and Italy to pay for eastern products.

Third, and perhaps most serious of all, was the financial burden of maintaining garrisons, factories, fleets and missions - for under the terms of the padroado real the Papacy had made the Portuguese crown responsible for financing all christian missions. The early voyages had been difficult to finance and private capital had been invited. Thereafter the crown sought to retain financial control and to reinvest its profits. Although no balance-sheet of the empire is possible and it cannot be clearly stated that the crown made a profit or loss overall in the sixteenth century, there is overwhelming evidence that there were frequent local shortages of funds both in Lisbon and throughout the stations of the empire, and these shortages could not then be met by the sophisticated financial expedients which are available to modern multi-national companies.

Could this royal trade monopoly have developed into the mercantile capitalism of the British or Dutch? What, after all, was essentially so different between the monopolistic state capitalism of Portugal and the monopolistic corporate capitalism of the Dutch? Yet Portuguese capitalism undeniably did fail to get launched and the reasons can be traced ultimately to a failure to overcome the problems of the initial stage of military and bureaucratic expansion. In particular failure can be attributed to the means that were employed to overcome the shortage of resources and which led to a predominance of feudalistic forms of government and society which were not conducive to saving and to reinvestment.

3. Manpower: Risk and the Problem of Recruitment

Portugal's shortage of material resources to facilitate expansion was matched by shortage of manpower. The voyages undertaken to the East are, where their details are known, horrific tales of suffering and endurance. Extremes of heat and cold, thirst and hunger were suffered in the small caravels, and when the great carracks were developed for the carreira da India the suffering was, if anything, increased. It was not uncommon for from one third to half of the human cargo to die in the course of a voyage. In 1576 an epidemic broke out in the fleet of the viceroy, Ruy Lourenco de Tavora, with the result that 900 out of a total of 1100 were dead on arrival at Mozambique.[1] As the century wore on more and more of the great carracks failed to complete their journeys and foundered, often with all hands, off the coasts of Africa. Between 1580 and 1620 approximately one carrack in every three was lost on the return from India. Once having reached the East the hazards remained. Of the 400 men who accompanied Cristovão da Gama into Ethiopia in 1540 only a few ever returned; of the 600 men with whom Francisco Barreto sailed for central Africa in 1569, barely 50 were left alive in 1573 when Barreto himself died.

How was it possible to recruit men for such expeditions? Could skilled artisans, soldiers and sailors be expected to enlist to face such hardships, with only their ordinary pay and the prospect of living under military discipline to tempt them? Still more important, where were officers to be found, and the literate and numerate men needed to staff the commercial bureaucracy which the crown sought to establish? Portugal simply did not produce the flood of graduates which the possession of thirty universities allowed Castile to pour into her imperial administration. Although the Jesuits founded a University at Evora, Portugal still largely depended on the single University of Coimbra to supply its educated manpower.

So the crown, unlike its Castilian counterpart, had to draw heavily on the military nobility to provide the leaders of the expeditions and to staff the bureaucracy. Not surprisingly the nobility imposed its own character on the empire, a character deriving from a system of military values very different from those required by the sort of careful commercial administration which the king wished to establish.

The early voyages in the Atlantic had been made by squires and knights from the households of the royal princes. The settlements in the islands and the wars against Morocco had likewise reflected the interests of this class, seeking land, employment and reputation. These fidalgos, initially mostly from the minor nobility, married into each other's families and went a long way towards turning the empire into the preserve of a small group of related clans. This tendency is in no way surprising. Kinship is a way by which skills, such as navigation, can be transmitted, and in most societies it is an established basis for trust, co-operation and mutual interest. However, ties of kinship can also exclude merit and reward demerit, and they are a means of creating monopolies of wealth and power. When a fidalgo from one of these families was appointed to an office, therefore, the crown was not appointing a salaried bureaucrat but was alienating its authority to a member of a clan with strongly articulated aristocratic and military values and interests.

Various devices were employed by the crown to try to exert some control over its officials. One was to move men around from office to office with considerable frequency; another was to appoint ecclesiastics to perform political or administrative functions, sometimes specifically as personal advisers of viceroys or commanders. A third device was to hold a judicial investigation into the conduct of an official. These inquiries were the counterpart of the Castilian residencia but they were not held automatically at the termination of a period in office as in Castile, and frequently the judges themselves behaved in a more scandalous fashion than the men they were investigating.

What of the rank and file? In many respects they resemble an organised, professional military force. They were paid, their names

were entered on muster-rolls and they enlisted for specified lengths
of time. They were subject to military discipline. Even so, Portuguese
forces in the East retained characteristics of an earlier type of military
organisation. The idea of personal service remained strong; a man
would enlist in the casa, or retinue of a great fidalgo and would have a
strong personal interest in loyalty to his commander. Although the
soldiers were paid by the crown, the captain under whom they served
would increase their pay from his own pocket and would often continue
to employ them after the campaigning season was over. As Linschoten
writes,

> 'There are likewise some Gentlemen that in winter time keepe
> open household for all soldiers that will come thether to
> meate ... Some souldiers have a Gentleman or Captaine to
> their friendes which lendeth them money to apparell them-
> selves withall, to the end when summer time commeth, they
> may be ready to goe with them in Fleet to sea, as also to
> have their friendship by night and at other times to beare
> them company, or to helpe them to bee revenged ... ' [2]

A similar hierarchy of service existed among junior officers and
officials. A man rose in the service of an important commander or
ecclesiastic on whom he depended for patronage, and seldom simply in
the service of the crown.

Recruitment of native-born Portuguese was never easy. Ships
companies were often made up by emptying the orphanages and prisons,
condemned criminals being regularly sent out to undertake dangerous
missions but with the possibility of working their remission. Once in
the East, the depleted crews could be completed by purchasing slaves
in Mozambique or by enlisting Asiatic seamen.

4. Predatory Nature of the Portuguese Empire

Early Portuguese expansion had been predatory in character.
Ships commissioned by the royal princes had hunted for seals,
plundered Moorish shipping or raided the African coast for slaves.
Men who participated sought to acquire fortunes as much by military
action as by peaceful trade which explains their preference for costly
attacks on Moroccan towns to the perils of trading voyages. In West
Africa the Portuguese had possessed certain valued entrepreneurial
skills, but in the Indian Ocean they ran great risks even to reach the
trading areas and once there found they had no particular skills to
offer and no goods to trade. Military supremacy, however, they did
have, provided for them by heavy artillery mounted on ships. This
sort of armament, unknown in the East, provided them with the sort of
military superiority which steel weapons and horses conferred on the
Castilians in America. As the expeditions were commanded by military

men it is not surprising that the potential of this military superiority
was early appreciated.

From the first, therefore, as with their Castilian contemporaries
in America, plundering the commercial wealth of the eastern cities
took precedence over attempts to trade, and with successful plunder
flourished the mentality of the plunderer. In pursuit of extremes of
wealth, extremes of human cupidity, cruelty and daring came into play.
Like the conquistadores in the mountains, jungles and deserts of
America, the Portuguese would endure any danger or hardship in the
search for instant and fabulous wealth; but he would not endure patient
toil in the trading factory or at the accounting desk. It was the mentality of the gambler or the gold prospector, not that of the businessman.
The pursuit of plunder kept together the retinues and attracted men to
serve under successful captains and viceroys. It was the movement of
the plunder frontier which attracted men to ever-new regions and to
make further discoveries. In other words plunder was the prime
motive force of 'discovery'.

However, the pursuit of plunder was not just for the fulfilment
of private ambition. It explains how the Portuguese empire in the
early days was financed and supplied and how it entered the commerce
of the East. The importance of the role played by plunder explains why
the Portuguese commercial empire represented at best merely an
embryonic form of capitalism and professionalisation and why it always
showed a tendency to revert to forms of landed and bureaucratic
feudalism.

5. Plunder and Individual Wealth

During the first two decades of the sixteenth century, the
Portuguese commanders in the Indian Ocean sacked or laid under
tribute all the coastal cities from Malacca to Mozambique. Only into
the Bay of Bengal they did not venture at this time. Although these
attacks had a long-term objective related to the establishment of a
commercial monopoly, they in fact amounted to the systematic stripping, by a highly organised band of pirates, of the accumulated wealth
of many centuries of trade. Unlike the Castilian conquistadores the
Portuguese largely confined their raids to the sea-coasts and seldom
damaged directly the inland communities which generated the trading
wealth, but in each case plunder was an almost essential ingredient of
their activities in order to acquire the resources on which military and
imperial expansion could take place. Piracy can be a way in which
capital is accumulated rather than dispersed and it is important to
establish how the Portuguese organised the plundering of the east and
what was done with the loot thus acquired.

In 1505 Dom Francisco de Almeida, the first viceroy, stormed

Mombasa. We are told that he dissuaded his men from pursuing the Sultan into the bush and

> 'changed their eagerness for this attack into eagerness
> to sack the town, which he divided among the different
> captains that they might prevent any disorder being
> committed. As nothing had been disturbed, there were
> such quantities of moveable goods in the town that they
> filled the king's palace and the open space in front with
> the first booty of that day, and obtained an equal quantity
> on the following day, but Dom Francisco would not allow
> them to take this booty on board for fear of the ships being
> overloaded, nor would he allow them to carry away the
> thousand prisoners that were captured but only two hundred,
> whom he divided among the noblemen.' [3]

Almeida had received strict instructions about the handling of plunder, in anticipation of the very real problems that arose after a victory. His instructions laid it down that when a prize was taken all trade-goods were to be made over to the factor and, as for the rest,

> 'albeit there should be no share in the prizes you make ...
> since everyone receives wages, we are nevertheless pleased
> to do them grace and to have it done in this manner.' [4]

So the crown recognised from the start that its men would not serve just for their wages. More had to be offered to attract sufficient officers and men. The division was to be as follows. When a prize was taken, the viceroy was to take a 'jewel' for himself up to the value of 500 cruzados and then 20% of what remained. The remaining four-fifths were to be divided into three parts. Two of these (more than half the total) were to be devoted to the financing of the royal fleets, the remainder (four-fifteenths of the total) was to be distributed in a carefully graded manner. The viceroy received 25 shares, each captain 10 shares and so down to the single share of the ordinary seaman. Ten shares finally were to be set aside for the church - in this case for the building of the Jeronimos monastery at Belem near Lisbon. [5] However, there was little chance of the plundering of a city proceeding in such an orderly manner. The king was told that if all those who had hidden their loot after the capture of Mombasa were to be punished then almost every Portuguese in the East would be under arrest. A more rough and ready way, therefore, was to divide a captured city into quarters to be allotted to different captains to plunder.

The crown was right to anticipate trouble. The foundering of boats overloaded with plunder is frequently recorded, and when Tristan da Cunha sacked Oja in 1507 many men were burnt in fires they had themselves started. Any delay in the share-out could also be disastrous and the following story explains much about the workings of

Portugal's military organisation and about the real absence of a
disciplined, salaried body of professionals to work the royal monopoly.
When Albuquerque exacted a ransom of 20,000 xerafins from Ormuz
in 1507, he tried to reserve the money for the supply of the fleet and
for the royal treasury. His officers and men considered some of this
to be their spoil and mutiny broke out. Albuquerque first offered to
deposit the money until the viceroy could decide and then offered to
make a provisional distribution. This was not satisfactory and one of
his captains told him frankly that he had better distribute the loot if he
wanted the loyalty of his men. Unable to agree, three of the mutinous
captains then sailed to lay charges against Albuquerque before the
viceroy. From this the great commander learned a lesson and after
future actions was meticulous about distributing the prizes.

The commanders and captains of the early Portuguese voyages
to the east thus stood to make enormous fortunes, but it is only
occasionally that the full extent of these becomes clear. Typical of the
smaller fry was Duarte de Lemos, captain of Mozambique from 1508-9,
and an assiduous fortune hunter, who went cruising to collect 'tribute'
along the Swahili coast. A letter reaching the king in 1510 spoke of
'much stealing from the prizes taken by the fleet of Duarte de Lemos
... and that Duarte de Lemos took as his share from the prize of a
sambuk 4,000 arrateis (an arratel is approximately a pound) of blood-
stones worth a great deal of money'. Off Socotra Lemos fell in with
Francisco de Pantoja who had just taken the Meri, a 600 ton Indian
merchant ship and one of the richest prizes of the age. Lemos duly
sequestered the share of the prize money that should have belonged to
Albuquerque.

Of the great commanders, the fortune-hunting success of Vasco
da Gama is best known. He commanded the first fleet to India in
1497-9, sailed again in 1502 and subsequently became viceroy in 1524,
dying in office. He came from an obscure fidalgo family but died as
Conde de Vidigueira, lord of Vidigueira and Vila de Frades, and the
possessor of an immense fortune. Much of this he owed to royal favour.
After his first India voyage he received 20,000 gold cruzados and the
right to sell 10 quintals of spices; he was granted the perpetual right
to invest 200 cruzados in any voyage and to ship his goods free of charge.
Finally he was made commander of any India fleet he chose, and became
admiral for life. However, royal favour accounted for only a part of
his fortune. His cruise up the African coast during 1502 was singularly
profitable. At Kilwa he received a bribe of 10,000 cruzados and
presents from the Sultan worth 5,000 cruzados. At Melinde his son
received gifts valued at 10,000 cruzados and the cruise finished in a
highly satisfactory manner when an Indian ship was plundered of 25,000
cruzados and the raja of Cannanor gave da Gama a jewelled necklace.
If these amounts are taken at their face value, then in the space of two
months he received presents and plunder equal to about a quarter of
the annual revenue of Portugal.

Albuquerque, who commanded a fleet in 1503, raided Madagascar, East Africa and the Hadramaut in 1507 and was governor of India from 1509-1515, won the reputation for being a tough soldier to whose hands wealth did not stick. When, however, he returned from Malacca to Goa in 1511 his ship, the Flor de la Mar, foundered off Ceylon and, according to his biographer, 'there was lost the richest spoils that ever were seen since India had been discovered. '

What happened to this personal wealth accumulated during twenty years of plundering the East? Was it brought back to Portugal? Was it invested, and if so, how? Was it spent as fast and as conspicuously as it was acquired? At present none of these questions can be answered in any exact way, but in the chronicles there is enough anecdotal evidence at least to suggest an answer.

This personal wealth was spent and spent lavishly. The Portuguese governors, da Gama for instance, tried to rival Indian potentates in their display and the magnificence of their gifts and their retinues. At a humble level we know that the average Portuguese soldier tried to acquire the life-style of a gentleman so that in 1524 da Gama had to issue sumptuary laws and to prevent his men bringing their pages with them on campaign. Indeed it was the maintenance of retinues of clients that appears to have consumed much of the wealth amassed. When Francisco Barreto, for instance, was forced to winter in Mozambique in 1547 he maintained the whole of his fleet at his own personal expense. In this way, a system of clientage, carried forward from medieval Portugal, was perpetuated with the inevitable result that the direct authority of a distant crown weakened in the shadow of the immediate prestige of the great lords. Charity and the church were another form of conspicuous expenditure. Manuel de Sousa Sepulveda, who died in the wreck of the Sao Joao in 1552, 'had spent more than 50,000 cruzados in India on giving food to many people, and on the good works he did to many men.' Another example is that of Dom Jeronimo Mascarenhas, captain of Cochin, who spent his fortune on building the Jesuit church of the Bom Jesus in Goa.

The profits of plunder were also invested in office. As shown in a later section, this movement into office-holding and into the purchase of trading rights was a natural extension of the habits of plunder and continued down an evolutionary path that was to restrict the economic development of the Portuguese empire.

6. Plunder as a Means of Breaking into Markets

It is clear from the crown's instructions to its commanders, that plunder was not seen just as an inevitable result of indiscipline and personal greed. It was also a deliberate policy. Almeida was instructed on reaching Sofala in 1505 to

'take all Moorish merchants who may be there from
foreign parts and all the gold and merchandise you
will find upon them. '

Similar instructions were issued to other commanders. In 1507, for
instance, Fernão Soares was told

'if , with the help of Our Lord, you were to find any
prizes or eminent merchants, you shall take them with
you ... to ransom and to profit by them in the best way
suited to our service. '

The counterpart of plunder was protection, and commanders were
instructed to spare those coastal rulers who would acknowledge
Portuguese overlordship and pay tribute. What, then, was the
objective of this policy, beyond a simple assertion of Portuguese
power? The clue lies in one of Almeida's instructions with regard to
rulers forced to pay tribute. He was told

'if you could pledge them to pay a regular tribute in
supplies and merchandise, this would be more to our
service. '

The plundering of Muslim ships and towns, therefore, not only
destroyed the trade of their rivals but provided the Portuguese with
the goods necessary for them to trade on their own account and so
provide both profit and the means to maintain their troops and warships.
For instance, after the storming of Kilwa in 1505 plunder was sent to
the royal factor at Sofala who valued this contribution at 13,000
mithqals; Mombasa also yielded 'cotton cloth from Cambay ... and in
this way the captain-major gathered a great sum for the Sofala trade.'
This became a regular practice for the Portuguese commanders in the
first two decades of the century. Merchant ships were waylaid,
usually between India and the Red Sea, the captains and crews took
their share and the merchandise was then consigned to the represen-
tative of the royal factory, where it would be used to purchase spices
in the Indian markets.

Inevitably, however, this use of plunder to supply trading stock
was not a policy that needed to be pursued once the Portuguese were
established in local trade and once the system of licences for Asiatic
traders was fully effective.

7. Plunder and the Supply of Fleets and Armies

Throughout the sixteenth century the Portuguese in the East
maintained military and naval forces permanently on a war footing.
By the standards of the seventeenth and eighteenth centuries these

forces were not large. Albuquerque commanded 600 men for the
attack on Malacca though Joao de Castro may have commanded as
many as 3,000 men at the relief of Diu in 1546. However, the small
size of these forces is deceptive for the Portuguese maintained
permanent garrisons scattered throughout the Indian Ocean and at the
end of the century two permanent war fleets escorted merchantmen
and fought off pirates along the north and south coasts of India
respectively. At the same time they were garrisoning a dozen coastal
towns in Morocco and were in a state of almost continuous war in
North Africa. They were also committed, after 1571, to large-scale
intervention in Angola and the Congo. Maintaining these forces
naturally imposed great strains on the empire's finances.

One way of paying for war, however, was to make it pay for
itself, a common enough idea for military men in the sixteenth century.
Thus the accounts of the fortress of Sofala for 1506 record the capture
of a dhow laden with

> 'one hundred bales of beans and one bale of lentils and
> eleven bales of unhusked rice'

all of which was handed over to the factor for 'the maintenance of the
people of the fortress.' The tribute demanded from local rulers was,
as often as not, taken in kind rather than cash. Thus Baticala in
western India agreed to pay 2,000 bags of rice annually and the natives
of Socotra were expected to show their loyalty to the tune of 600 sheep.
Mafia paid tribute in the form of pitch and coir used for rope making.
Even so, the maintenance of the fleets was a major problem. Having
occupied Aden harbour briefly in 1513 Albuquerque

> 'ordered all the masters of the ships to refit them with
> rigging and shrouds, and all other things they are in
> need of, out of the ships of the Moors ... and to strip
> them of all the merchandise which they carried, and
> gather together all the provisions they could find.' [6]

Measures such as these would be taken by any prudent commander but
there is abundant evidence that the Portuguese conquistadores came
to expect their expeditions to pay for themselves and frequently justified them simply on the grounds that they were essential to keep up the
supply of cash and provisions for the fleet. When Vasco da Gama
first proposed to the king that a fleet be left permanently in Indian
waters he justified it by saying that

> 'the expenditure that they would incur at sea would be
> gained by prizes that they would make'. [7]

It was Albuquerque, however, who was the chief exponent of this
policy, as he was also the chief architect of Portuguese power in the

East. During his cruise along the Arabian coast in 1507, he had used
plunder to pay his men's wages and after the first attack on Ormuz
had made up arrears to the amount of 15,000 <u>cruzados</u>. Later he was
to write to the king of the problems that would arise if peace broke
out, and of a possible solution that might be found in the selling of
safe-conducts. He was to justify his second attack on Ormuz in 1515
by writing

> 'I saw how great would be my need and shame if I did not
> capture some place wherein to provide the fleet with supplies.'

and he chose Ormuz because it would yield

> 'one hundred and twenty thousand <u>xerafins</u> in cash, with the
> tribute due to us ... and this without trouble.' [8]

8. The Movement of the Plunder Frontier

If, as has been suggested, the gambler's expectation of sudden
riches to be obtained by plunder explains the excessive hardships
undergone and the exceptional daring shown by the conquistadores, and
if plunder influenced the shape of Portuguese society in the East and
the type of administrative structure that emerged, then tensions were
bound to arise once the accumulations of wealth discovered on first
arrival had been dispersed. This situation can be seen most clearly
in the Spanish advance in America where the exhaustion of the areas
already plundered drove the conquistadores on to fresh conquests.
Moreover Spanish conquests virtually ceased once the limits of settled
Indian society had been reached in the middle of the sixteenth century
and there were no further accumulations of bullion to be looted.

There was a similar movement of the plunder frontier in
Portugal's advance in the East. The plundering of East Africa can be
said to have been over by 1523 when the last successful piratical raid
was mounted against the Querimba Islands. Similarly by about 1520
the piratical raids on the other Indian Ocean seaboard cities ended and
the Portuguese themselves acquired vested interests best protected by
peace and an orderly conduct of affairs. The plunder frontier then
moved further East.

The first Portuguese expeditions into Indonesia date from 1511;
Ceylon was forced to pay a massive tribute and accept a Portuguese
force in Columbo in 1518 and in 1517 the first Portuguese 'embassy' to
China opened an era of piracy in the Far East. This second era of
plunder lasted till the middle of the century to be gradually replaced in
its turn by more settled trade conditions; Macao was founded about 1557
and trade with Japan developed soon afterwards. In 1559 the first
Portuguese protectorate over Kotte in Ceylon was established.

With the closing of the frontier, what replaced plunder in the structure of the Iberian empires? The era of conquest had created expectations and patterns of behaviour which persisted when the conquests were over. For two generations the Portuguese in the East had expected to make themselves rich by their military prowess. Although they were prepared to spend their wealth and even to invest it, they tended to treat it more as a gambler's stake than as a businessman's investment. They won it not through demeaning toil but through the honourable exercise of arms. These values and assumptions, present in medieval Europe, were carried over into modern times in the notion of dérogeance but they received added strength and confirmation through contact with eastern society with its strong caste traditions and its employment of slaves for menial labour.

According to a pattern familiar enough in European history, the military class, deprived of opportunities to obtain rewards in warfare, turned instead to the feudal profits of land-holding and office which often amounted to little more than the institutionalised plunder of the surplus wealth of the productive classes of society.

9. Land-holding and Office in the Portuguese Empire

The founders of the empire had warned against acquiring territorial empire. Indeed they intended all Portuguese to live under military discipline within the confines of forts or factories. Yet, as the century wore on, and particularly in the second half, the Portuguese embarked more and more on territorial enterprises. Why was this so?

To a certain extent the acquisition of territory should be seen in connection with the free-lance activity of Portuguese deserters, pirates and mercenaries. As early as 1510 during the battles around Goa, Portuguese renegades were to be found fighting for the sultan of Bijapur and, significantly, trying to lure their compatriots to desert with promises of rewards and riches in Indian service. In 1515 Albuquerque captured and burnt some renegades at Ormuz and at Mombasa in 1505 the Portuguese were fired on by guns worked by deserters. The factor of Sofala wrote in 1511 that Portuguese deserters were setting themselves up in the interior and that one had married a daughter of a local king. As Portugal's own wars of conquest died down, free-lance military service with African or Asian potentates acquired added attractions. The activities of some of these pirates and mercenaries have been vividly described in the autobiography of Fernao Mendes Pinto.

One of the rewards sought by these men was land on which to settle or some equivalent source of wealth in slaves, women, cattle or tribute. Frequently they were so rewarded and became respected members of eastern ruling élites. To counter this desertion the viceroys had to be able to reward their followers in similar fashion.

There were, however, additional pressures for the acquisition of land. One of these was the need for security. This may have been the motive behind the annexation of the Goan provinces and of the coastal territories of Daman and Bassein known as the provincia do norte. It may also have been the motive behind the decision to conquer Ceylon in the 1590s, at a time when the rise of Mughal power and other problems appeared to threaten Portugal's survival in India proper. On the other hand, the invasion of Zambesia in 1569 was motivated by a desire to emulate Pizarro and conquer the mines which were the source, it was believed, of African gold and silver.

Present also were considerations which in the earlier part of the century had dictated the policy of plunder. The royal treasury needed funds, the royal factors needed access to the products and crafts of the land, missionaries wanted converts and individual Portuguese increasingly sought rewards which the imperial machine could no longer satisfy. Instead of the expansion of the Portuguese armed forces enabling the crown to develop a commercial empire, the need to maintain and satisfy these forces now dictated that it should establish a land empire. So a landed empire was acquired, modest by Castilian standards, but nonetheless considerable. Areas in north-western India, Goa, Ceylon, the Moluccas and Zambesia came under Portuguese rule, as did extensive areas of west African territory, now known as Angola.

The forms of 'land' grant developed in the east bore much greater resemblance to the encomienda of the Spanish conquests than to the landed estates of Europe. The encomienda was a grant of Indians whose tribute, and sometimes whose labour, was supposed to support the military obligations of the Spanish conquerors. In India the units are sometimes called pagodas which were the alienated revenues of Indian temples, but more usually they were aldeias: villages, assigned to an individual Portuguese, to a church or religious order, or to an office to provide a source of income. In Zambesia it appears that the Portuguese took over whole chieftaincies, not necessarily supplanting the chiefs but installing themselves as overlords.

These were not so much grants of land as grants of revenue from lands and in east Africa grants of jurisdiction also. Frequently a military obligation is implied in the terms of the grant. The holders of these grants obtained feudal payments from the inhabitants in cash, kind or service. While supporting a leisured class of Portuguese fidalgos, these territories also helped to meet the manpower problems of the Portuguese and to give them increased access to the products and skills of the land.

The other interest of the Portuguese fortune hunter was to acquire an important office; the captaincy of a vessel, command of a fort or factor in one of the royal factories.

There was an intimate and necessary connection between office holding and the maintenance of military forces. The Portuguese who contracted to serve the crown in the east did so, not just for their pay but with an expectation of future rewards. Records of the service of individuals were maintained in Goa and after a number of years a man would obtain a certificate setting out his services to the crown. This provided the basis on which he would then seek a reward either in the East by petitioning the viceroy or some other dignitary or back in Portugal where he would present himself at court armed with his certificate and with presents for the influential courtiers.

In recognition of his services a soldier expected to be granted an office or command. This expectation assumed in his mind almost the status of a contract, and in Peru the Castilian conquistadores were ultimately prepared to take up arms against the crown to defend the encomiendas they claimed as their reward. Failure to secure adequate reward was sometimes the occasion for treason. When Fernao de Magalhaes renounced his allegiance to king Manuel and entered Castilian service in 1517 it was with an acute sense of grievance that his services had not received adequate recognition from the king. Offices were seen also as a form of pension to support a man in his old age or as provision for his dependants. It is very common for a widow or children to petition the crown for the grant of lands or offices as a reward for the services of their dead husband and father. Without a ready supply of offices and lands, therefore, the whole military system of the Portuguese would cease to function.

Offices were always in short supply and the pressure of petitioners must certainly have been one of the forces behind the steady expansion of the empire. However, there was another, rather novel way of meeting the demands of petitioners and this was to create a waiting list for offices. By the end of the century many petitioners would find, on being granted an office, that there were half a dozen or more people ahead of them on the list 'so that if they doe procure the reversion of any office, it is so long before the time commeth that they doe enjoy them, beeing many in reversion, that oftentimes they die before they can obtaine them'.[9]

Although the Portuguese continued to believe that they had right to occupy the offices of the crown as a reward for their services, it was inevitable that an element of venality would creep into the system. The offices that were granted were not granted for life but only for a short period of three years. The office holders were under pressure to make a quick profit during their short tenure and had no incentive to husband the resources of their commands or sustain honest and painstaking administrative practices. In particular they took to breaking the royal trade monopoly which they were supposed to be upholding :

> 'for that the King, say they, gave them their offices, thereby to pay them for their services in times past, and not for the profit of the commonwealth.' [10]

The leaks in the royal monopolies grew to such proportions that the royal trade sometimes drained away entirely. In 1548 the factor at Sofala reported that scarcely a tusk had been traded at the royal factory while the captain, Jorge Telo de Meneses, had shipped 40,000 arrobas of ivory on his own private account. At Ormuz we are told that

> 'no man may buy, sel, ship or lade any ware, before the Captaine hath soulde, shipped, fraughted, and dispatched his wares away, not that he hath any such authoritie from the King for he wholy forbiddeth it, but they take such authoritie of themselves.' [11]

By the end of the century the king had decided to cut his losses and was prepared to sell part or all of his trading monopoly to the incoming captain. A system of venality thereby emerged. The offices were still granted as a result of petitions but the right to exercise the royal monopoly had to be paid for.

Just as plunder had been, in effect, the gambler's hopes for a quick killing from a single speculative investment, with very high risk being taken in the hope of very high reward, so also were the profits of offices speculative and short term; the major captaincies and the vice-royalty itself were three-year appointments, while commands like that of captain-major of the Japan voyage were for a single year only. Emphasis was placed on making quick fortunes, often by what in the twentieth century would be called 'asset stripping', and not on long term investment with low profits and a careful husbanding of resources. One example of this speculative mentality was the building of ever bigger and bigger vessels, until great 2,000 ton, thoroughly unseaworthy carracks were being constructed; ships of very high risk but, if safely brought into port, maximising the profits from the single voyage which their captain had bought.

Early in the sixteenth century the Portuguese discoveries in the Indian Ocean and the Orient encouraged the Portuguese crown to conceive of creating a vast state-run capitalistic trading enterprise, to be secured and policed by its own expanded armed forces and operated by its own salaried, professional bureaucracy. It sought to realise this concept in the early organisation of the empire in the East, but within a few years the practical difficulties of military and bureaucratic expansion in the shape of Portugal's shortage of resources and skilled manpower began to dictate other policies if such expansion was to be effected. The expansion of the Portuguese armed forces and bureaucracy was found to be possible only through engaging the Portuguese nobility in the enterprise, allowing them to recruit their own followers and so decentralising royal authority, and through sanctioning plunder, both as a means of attracting manpower and also providing the resources which Portugal itself lacked to equip and finance its military and imperial expansion.

The use of plunder to supply the fleets and factories and to reward the soldiers was, from the crown's viewpoint, a necessary but transient phase. However the expectations that it created in the minds of the fidalgo class were more enduring and the means at the crown's disposal to control such expectations were too few. In France, as the following article will show, the government brought plunder under control by increasing its bureaucratic surveillance of its armies and by creating a vast centrally-controlled magazine system which diminished both the need for plunder and the opportunity to plunder on foraging expeditions. Such an imposition of central government authority was impossible in Portugal's far flung empire and the Portuguese crown was forced instead to sublimate rather than discipline the expectations of its armed forces by offering rewards for their military service in land grants and office-holding. This was Portugal's wrong-turning in the Military Revolution and it produced harmful economic effects. In a bid to re-establish a degree of central control and also to secure some profit from its own empire the crown resorted first to granting offices on short tenures and then to leasing its trade on short leases. Both expedients however only encouraged the office-and lease-holders to exploit these assets while they had the chance. Short-term leases gave wealthy Portuguese the opportunity to invest in trade, but only with short-term investments. What this encouraged was highly speculative enterprises or the naked plundering of their commands by officials from the viceroy downwards.

By the end of the sixteenth century this pattern of social and economic behaviour had destroyed any burgeoning Portuguese capitalism and left the empire with all the strengths of a decentralized and locally deep-rooted feudalism, but without the financial reserves and central authority to further strengthen its armed forces for a long drawn-out struggle to survive in a new era of mercantile competition with the Dutch and English.

NOTES

1. A.C. Burnell and P.A. Tiele eds., The Voyage of John Huyghen van Linschoten to the East Indies, 2 vols., for the Hakluyt Society (London, 1884), 1, p.40.

2. Ibid, 1, pp.192,199.

3. Joao de Barros, Da Asia. Extract published in G.S.P. Freeman-Grenville, The East African Coast (Oxford, 1962), p.103.

4. 'Instructions to the Captain-major D. Francisco de Almeida', Documents on the Portuguese in Mozambique and Central Africa, vol.1 (Lisbon, 1962), pp.249-251.

5. This distribution can be compared with the agreements reached between crown and adelantado in the conquest of America. There the Castilian crown always took a fifth (the Portuguese crown aimed to take over half) and it was considered to be exceptional and somewhat presumptuous of Cortes to demand the equivalent for himself. In Almeida's case the viceroy received more than a fifth, but it was still less than the crown's share.

6. W. de Gray Birch ed., The Commentaries of the Great Afonso de Albuquerque, 4 vols., for the Hakluyt Society (London, 1875-84), 4, p.23.

7. H.E.J. Stanley ed., The Three Voyages of Vasco da Gama, for the Hakluyt Society (London, 1869), p.282.

8. Afonso de Albuquerque to King Manuel, 22/9/1515, Documents on the Portuguese ... , 4, p.237.

9. The Voyage of Linschoten ... , 1, p.203.

10. Ibid, 1, p.203.

11. Ibid, 1, p.54.

2. The Military Revolution and the Professionalisation of the French Army under the Ancien Régime*

COLIN JONES

The middle decades of the seventeenth century saw a shift in the centre of gravity of European dynastic politics from the Habsburgs to the Bourbons. The grandiose schemes of European dominance held by the combined Spanish and Imperial Habsburg power in the sixteenth century had foundered on the opposition of the Turks on one hand and the Dutch and their allies on the other. Even so, in the closing years of the century, Habsburg Spain had still been indisputably the greatest power in Europe, while France had been in eclipse, submerged in a welter of internal dissension which would last down to the Fronde (1648-1653). Nevertheless, in the Treaty of Westphalia in 1648 with the Imperial power and in the Treaty of the Pyrenees in 1659 with Spain, France was to assert its primacy in Europe. The resultant change in international ranking order derived above all from feats of arms. Spain had, it is true, developed grave internal problems which weakened its international standing; but its defeat was ultimately military and the French victory over the legendary Spanish tercios at Rocroi in 1643 had symbolically tolled the knell of Habsburg dominance in Europe.

It was France's army which lay at the nub of her newfound primacy of place in Europe: her navy in the 1640s and 1650s was still inconsiderable and was never to be ascribed more than a subaltern role in grand strategy. Successive Bourbon rulers and their principal ministers - Richelieu (1624-1642) and Mazarin (1642-1661) not least - managed to create an original and cogent blend of state power and military strength which, from the middle of the seventeenth century down to the end of the Ancien Régime in 1789 would enable France to aspire to European hegemony. This was an achievement which was intricately associated with profound changes which had been taking place since the late sixteenth century in the conduct of war. These changes, dubbed by Michael Roberts as a 'Military Revolution', significantly intensified the impact of warfare on the rest of society.[1] They also pointed logically towards the professionalisation of European armies. It is upon the pioneering role of the emergent absolutist monarchy in France in this process that this article will focus.

* Parts of this article have been extracted from the author's 'The Welfare of the French Foot-Soldier from Richelieu to Napoleon', History, 1980. They are reproduced here with the kind permission of the Editor of History.

1. The Initial Expansion of the Army: Recruitment and Supplies

The growth in the size of armies was perhaps the most obvious aspect of Europe's Military Revolution.[2] The Spanish army, for example, which had numbered 150,000 men in the 1550s had doubled in size by the 1630s; the Dutch Republic more than quintupled the size of its forces between the late sixteenth and late seventeenth centuries; and Sweden's army mushroomed from a mere 15,000 men in the 1590s to 100,000 men by the close of the seventeenth century. In France, the expansion was arguably even more sudden and abrupt than else-where. In the sixteenth century, the crown's army had rarely, and even then by little, exceeded 50,000 men. Indeed, on the death of Henri IV in 1610, numbers stood at less than 20,000 men and this figure was more or less maintained during the next couple of decades. Once Richelieu and Louis XIII had in 1635 thrown in France's lot against the Habsburgs in the Thirty Years War, however, the strength of the army grew rapidly to over 150,000 men. The rise in numbers continued after Richelieu's death in 1642 and from the last decades of the seventeenth century to the end of the Ancien Régime, the state had at least a quarter of a million soldiers on its books - and sometimes double that number in time of war. This sharp rise in numbers was all the more remarkable in that whereas hitherto most armies had been extensively dismantled at the end of each campaigning season, the new armies were primarily standing forces maintained on a quasi-permanent basis.

This quantum leap in the size of the French army was only made with the greatest difficulty especially in the early years. The admini-strative infra-structure of the armed forces which Richelieu and Louis XIII had inherited was unimpressive in the extreme and the sheer speed of the build-up in forces left no time for traditions of military administration to develop. Although the French army's later prestige was to be based upon centralised state control, it is important to recognize that, in the early stages, the fighting forces pitted against Spain had to be cobbled together with an almost prodigal delegation of powers. This was particularly apparent in the field of recruitment. The new army was a mixture of the most diverse elements. A great number of the troops - perhaps more than a third - were foreign mer-cenaries, for the most part brought over to the French side by their commanders. In 1636, for example, Richelieu had secured the support of some 20,000 foreign troops under the great military enterpriser Bernard of Saxe-Weimar. The ancient provincial militias of the frontier regions and the bourgeois militias of the towns were pres-surised into providing contingents of men to fight alongside such mer-cenaries in the war emergency of the late 1630s. The feudal levy - repeated periodically down to the 1690s - also brought some men to the standards. The bulk of foot-soldiers, however, were recruited through a system of more or less voluntary enlistment. What normally happened was that the crown granted a commission to a regimental commander - a colonel - who in return undertook to supply an agreed number of men. To make up the required numbers, colonels sold the posts of company-commanders - captains - to the highest bidders. Captains, the colonels themselves, or on occasion special recruiting officers (<u>racoleurs</u>) appointed by the commanders, set about raising the numbers by whatever means seemed most effective. Commanders who were seigneurs - and most were - could count on enlisting peasants from their estates during the winter months; otherwise any method of obtaining recruits was fair enough, even if it meant raiding prisons and hospitals. If the men who were enlisted were, in their different ways, 'serving the king', their prime allegiance was likely to be to their captains and colonels. Even royal muster rolls referred to the men as 'soldat du sieur (X), capitaine au régiment de (Y)'. Not until 1745 was this formula changed to a more impersonal form.

The colonels and captains who played such a notable part in recruitment procedures in the early seventeenth century were also responsible for many of their troops' supplies and provisions. Each new recruit was entitled to a bounty from the royal treasury. This, along with the men's wages, was normally paid to their commanders who were permitted to deduct various sums which represented the cost of food, equipment and other ancillary services. Many commanders, for example, provided their men with a suit of clothing - scarcely a uniform as yet - and any arms and ammunition they were to have. Commanders were also responsible for establishing the military hospitals and chaplaincies which a royal edict of 1629 had introduced. For many of the supplies, commanders relied on contracts which either they or the central government made with civilian entrepreneurs. Given the only very rudimentary supervision which the government could exercise over armies in the field, these arrangements strongly favoured corruption and peculation on the part of commanders and contractors. Both stood to make considerable profits at the expense of the troops on one hand and the state on the other.

There was a variety of ways in which commanders and contractors could turn warfare into a profitable entrepreneurial exercise. They could, firstly, economise on the services they were theoretically bound to supply. Clothing and food often arrived late or not at all, or was of poor quality. The regimental hospitals, theoretically introduced in 1629, were in practice rarities well into the 1640s and 1650s. Secondly, commanders could charge excessively for those services they did supply - bills for expenses would be met out of the wages fund, for example, rather than out of the pockets of commanders. Thirdly, commanders were prone to withhold part or even all of the men's wages. Finally, commanders could defraud the government by putting in requests for payment for a fictitious number of troops. The government fixed the wage-bill of each regiment after a periodic muster at which it was notoriously easy to swell numbers with soldiers borrowed from other regiments, camp-followers, servants on the retinue of the officers and the local inhabitants. So numerous were 'paper recruits' (passe-volants) that one historian has calculated that the effective strength of the seventeenth-century army may well have been as much as a third inferior to the numbers on paper.[3]

The virtual absence of solidly-based state-controlled military institutions allowed such fraudulent practices to flourish as never before. Networks of financial, commercial and familial relations linked commanders, contractors and personages close to the centre of government in business cartels which made the fortunes of their members through cheating the state. There were, moreover, no keener enthusiasts of this form of activity than Richelieu and Mazarin who both flagrantly utilised their key position in the king's counsels as a means of personal enrichment. In addition, the notorious parsimony of the government in regard to its army also encouraged corruption. The huge standing army with which the state was waging war from the 1630s was immensely expensive and governments were obliged to have recourse to a plethora of extreme financial policies - tax-rises, creations of venal offices, the floating of huge loans, devaluations, revaluations, and the like - in order to ensure that their armed forces remained in the field. In such fevered financial circumstances, the state often looked on the pay of the men as more of a luxury than a necessity. Moreover, in order to save money the government periodically disbanded some of the newer regiments - which formed the majority - before their commanders had had sufficient time to amortize the investment they had made in purchasing a commission. This governmental stratagem inevitably had the effect of whetting commanders' appetites for a fast return on outlay by whatever means lay at hand.

2. The Initial Expansion of the Army: Incentives

The most frequent victim of the whirligig of corruption and the cut-throat competition for fast profits and big savings which characterised the military machine created in the second quarter of the seventeenth century was the well-being of the soldiers. The increased size of the army presented unparallelled problems of control - not least of sanitary control. With regimental infirmaries still little more than a pipe-dream, for example, medical aid tended to be forthcoming either from charitably-disposed barber-surgeons on the retinue of the officers; from local quacks or charlatans; or from the prostitutes and camp-followers who were called on to justify their existence from time to time by acting as unpaid nurses. Health conditions were primitive in the extreme, especially in military camps, deaths in which always far exceeded deaths in battle: 'A body of troops which camps cannot remain for long in the same place', stated one government report in the early seventeenth century, 'without an extreme infection occurring as a consequence of the dirtiness of the soldiers, the horses which die there and the beasts slaughtered'.[4]

Disease was thus a frequent visitor to the camps of the army, and there combined with the effects of exposure to climatic extremes and the hunger which might arise when supplies or wages failed to materialise. It was little wonder that armies were important vectors of disease: most critically of plague, most frequently perhaps of syphilis, as well as of the dreaded 'camp fever' - the generic name given to a wide variety of infectious diseases including typhus, typhoid fever and dysentery. Scurvy also caused much damage - testimony to the poor diet of the troops. Pulmonary and respiratory diseases, skin ailments and sores, rheumatism, gout, hernias and premature senility also took their toll.

Given this litany of misery and woe - as well as the fact that wages were low or non-existent and that chances of promotion were probably slim - it may seem somewhat surprising that the state was able to increase the size of its armed forces as rapidly as it did in the 1630s. It is true that a large number of passe-volants and an exceptionally high desertion rate may distort the extent of the build-up. It is also true that civilian life in this period was stark and miserable and might offer fewer employment opportunities than the army - particularly now it was a standing army. Nevertheless, it would appear that by far the greatest incentive to recruitment was the opportunity for plunder which warfare then permitted.

Pillage - 'Mademoiselle Picorée' in army slang - constituted, along with women and drink, the unofficial wages of war. It was a form of activity at which the authorities connived or even shared. For Richelieu, for example, plunder by the troops was to be tolerated if only because it comprised 'an encouragement for the soldiers to do better'.[5] It formed a sort of military cement which kept armies together especially during the long sieges with which the wars of the period were replete. It was, significantly, when the prospect of plunder disappeared that desertion rates were liable to rise. Theft and violent crime in the towns, banditry and highway-robbery in the hills might offer alternative forms of subsistence and enrichment in which both officers and men could deploy their martial arts.

The perpetual financial embarrassment of the government in the early seventeenth century helped to generalise the practice of plunder. A single delay in state income from taxes or the borrowing process - a tax-revolt, for example, or an unexpected piece of financial jiggery-pokery - could trigger off a failure of supply which left the armies in the field little option but to live off their wits. Louis XIV's great military engineer Vauban, for example, could remember going three weeks in the field in his younger days without a single food convoy reaching his detachment. In such circumstances, plunder was an unavoidable necessity. It mattered little whether the indigenous population was friend or foe. Although it was desirable that the troops should, in the current military jargon, 'maintain themselves at the expense of the enemy', hungry soldiers were likely to pillage French peasants as cruelly and mercilessly as they might German, Italian or Spanish ones.

Open looting was only the least organised of a whole spectrum of techniques by which the army extracted its means of subsistence from the civilian population. Although no one - even their officers - could count themselves immune from the troops' penchant for pillage, it was usually the least privileged and therefore most defenceless part of the civilian population who suffered most from military depredations. It was they who, in the first place, paid the lion's share of the taxes which went to support the newly-expanded army. They also bore the brunt of troop billeting. In the absence of centrally-administered barracks or garrisons, troops were billeted on private households which were obliged by law to provide shelter, bedding, food, cooking utensils, heating, lighting and salt. This was an extremely heavy burden - more than one authority accounted it as even heavier than the conventional tax burden. It could drag on for months, moreover, when a detachment was 'wintering' in a region awaiting the opening of the campaigning season in Spring. Besides the statutory obligations of the civilian hosts, the latter also had to bear with the whims and petty violence of their uninvited armed guests. Immediate gratification did not exhaust the appetite of the troops for pillage. Camp-followers and military suppliers acted as middle-men in the creation of markets for booty. Treasures, foodstuffs, livestock, farm equipment, even prisoners and civilians held to ransom - all was grist to the booty mill. Transmuted into cash, such spoils allowed the formation of private capital which, provided the soldier was provident and that he survived his war days, might do something to compensate for the rigours of military life. Helpful in this respect too was the so-called 'Contribution System' from which the men benefited. This glorified system of 'protection money', already exploited by Portuguese commanders in the Indian Ocean in the sixteenth century, had been popularised in Europe in the 1620s and 1630s by the great German mercenary commander Wallenstein. Under its provisions a town or village agreed to levy a sum with which to purchase from passing troops an exemption from direct plunder.

The prevalence of plunder was not of course new. Its precepts and practices had long been codified: there was little that the Italian Renaissance condottiere or his overseas equivalent, the Portuguese or Spanish conquistador, had not devised before the French line regiment of the Thirty Years' War. What was new, however, was the scale of the impact which the sprawling and decentralised new armies could make on civilian populations. The strain was all the greater where the men sought enrichment as well as subsistence. In addition, the beleaguered, over-taxed and ill-treated agricultural producer had to contend with the often desperate violence and criminality of huge numbers of camp-followers in the train of any army. Ex-soldiers and deserters in particular formed a marginal and rootless element in war zones whose lawlessness repressive government legislation vainly attempted to curb. The cumulated sum of war damage could thus be considerable. Population losses - in a labour-intensive agricultural system, a rough and ready quantitative index of minimum damage - were often sizeable. The presence of royal armies in the Paris region during the Fronde caused the reduction of the indigenous population by about a fifth. Lorraine was even worse affected: Jacques Callot, the artist of horrors of early seventeenth century warfare, was a Lorrainer and Saint Vincent de Paul used the area as a laboratory for his charitable experiments in the 1630s and early 1640s. Certain areas there and in neighbouring Franche-Comté lost between two-thirds and three-quarters of their population during the course of the Thirty Years' War, and the traumatic war experiences marked a profound caesura in the social and economic development of both provinces.

It was thus little wonder that the mere arrival of troops in an area could trigger off a mass exodus of frightened peasants. The numerous popular revolts of the period also bear witness to a less resigned form of resentment against the military and the state that it underpinned. Whatever the determination of rebels, however, the huge and undisciplined army made a very effective policing agency. Indeed, the very threat of the appearance of troops was on occasion enough to induce spontaneous docility in populations angry with tax innovations.

3. The Rationale of State Centralisation

In spite of the evident advantages of having the army, through widespread plundering and through its more licit tax-extractive activities, pay for its own upkeep, there eventually came a point at which the operations of the ill-disciplined military seemed self-defeating. Governments increasingly receptive to mercantilistic arguments, for example, began to realise that the army, by crippling the subsistence-orientated economy of the majority of Frenchmen, was killing the goose that laid the golden eggs. If the fighting strength of the state really did depend, as the mercantilists suggested, upon the solidity of its financial and economic institutions, then it was crucial that these institutions be properly protected and nurtured. This was particularly true after the signing of peace with the Spanish in 1659. Peace put an end to the continued possibility of living at the expense of the enemy and highlighted the need for the development of more rational forms of exploitation of the nation's resources.

There were moreover powerful military arguments in favour of closer state controls over the kind of wildcat private enterprise which had dominated military institutions in the early seventeenth century. Failures of discipline and supply had on occasion reduced the effectiveness of the army in the field. As Richelieu learned to his cost,

'History knows more armies ruined by want and disorder
than by the efforts of their enemies'.[6]

In the late 1630s, the young Turenne had kept the French army intact
on the German front only by selling off his family pewter and placing
his personal credit at the disposal of his army's suppliers. When the
state's cheques bounced, the military machine could falter. The collapse of France's expedition in the Valtelline in 1637, for example,
was directly linked to a delay in levying a forced loan on French towns.
A question-mark also came to hang over the customary toleration of
indiscriminate plundering. On frequent occasions - most notoriously
in the indiscipline which French troops were to display in the invasion
of the Palatinate in 1689 - plunder revealed itself less as a cohesive
element among the troops than as a military solvent. The growth in
the size of armies also placed too heavy a load on many areas where it
proved simply impossible to extract sufficient to feed the troops. This
in turn necessitated sending men further and further afield on foraging
expeditions. When times were hard, this was tantamount to encouraging desertion.

High desertion rates could not be tolerated in a period in which
discipline and training on the field of battle seemed the passport to
military success. The growing facility which generals after Gustavus
Adolphus displayed in handling large numbers of men on the battlefield,
the intensification of fire-power as a result of improvements in fire-
arm technology and the growing prevalence of linear tactical formations on the battlefield all placed a premium on having an army which
was not only large but was also sufficiently well-drilled to obey orders
swiftly and unflinchingly. Trained and battle-hardened troops became
a much sought-after item of military hardware. The master-tactician
of eighteenth-century warfare, the Marshal de Saxe, was indeed to
maintain, as a logical consequence of this, that the sign of truly intel-
ligent generalship was to go through one's entire military career
without fighting a single battle. As he advised on another occasion:

'It is better to put off the attack for several days than to
expose oneself to losing rashly a single grenadier: he has
been twenty years in the making'.[7]

Increasingly, therefore, military requirements were for a better-
trained and more well-disciplined soldier - of a type which only the
state had the resources or indeed the incentive to create.

From about the middle of the seventeenth century, other factors
were favouring the limitation of private enterprise within the army and
the increase of state intervention in all spheres of military administration. Any state - and a fortiori a supposedly absolutist one -
requires its orders to be obeyed. To the extent therefore that many of
the reforms aimed merely to correct abuses, there was an inbuilt bias

towards centralisation once the over-arching authority of the state was better established - as was the case from the personal reign of Louis XIV onwards. Military reform could also have salutary political consequences. Closer controls over the noble officer corps, for example, helped defuse the constitutional and political threat which, as the Fronde demonstrated, independently-minded and discontented grandees still posed the state. Questions of finance also lay close to the heart of the government's thinking on the issue of military reform. It could scarcely escape attention that under the old scheme of things, the pockets of colonels, captains and contractors were being lined at the direct expense of the state treasury. It was symptomatic of the general drift of reform that the so-called 'Contribution System' was not done away with but was now run by the government bureaucracy rather than by commanders in the field. The state was not against fleecing enemy populations; but it wished to end arbitrary plundering done on home soil, and to ensure that the state took the biggest cut of any proceeds.

4. The Formation of the State Bureaucracy

The tightening of state control over the military establishment would have been unthinkable without the formation of the parallel institutions characteristic of the absolutist state. The colossal sums of money required for the state to prosecute warfare on a regular basis and on a new and massive scale had been organised, initially at least, by a formidable array of emergency measures, whose general effect had been the delegation of powers. In much the same way that the new army had been recruited and supplied largely by private enterprise, so, for example, direct taxes were placed in the hands of officiers, officials who purchased their posts and even, on payment of an annual sum known as the paulette, could dispose of them as pieces of private property; while indirect taxes were farmed out to similarly independent traitants and partisans. That the ranks of the new bureaucracy were frequently called upon to place their personal credit at the disposal of the state merely typified the amalgam of ingenuity and desperation which constituted French financial policy in this critical period. It could not, however, obscure the problems of central control which the sprawling new bureaucracy posed.

Much of the administrative machinery introduced in the early seventeenth century remained more or less intact down to the end of the Ancien Régime. With only very limited financial resources at its disposal, for example, the state simply could not have afforded to have bought itself out of its dependence on the prodigious numbers of venal officials in the new bureaucracy - any more, indeed, than it dared risk alienating the nobility by drumming them out of the officer corps in the new army. In order to check and counteract the centrifugal forces which the state had unleashed within its own administration, however, the monarchy began to develop the system of commissaires. These were

royal officials appointed by the crown for specific tasks and their commissions were revocable at will. The Intendant, the best-known of all
the types of commissaires, came to represent the very quintessence of
strong central control. In particular, the Intendant de police, justice
et finances appointed eventually to every généralité acted as the
'administrative factotum'[8] of the crown, supervising, controlling and
where necessary duplicating the activities of the other layers of the
bureaucracy and acting virtually as royal viceroy to each province.

It was eloquent of the blend of military and civilian functions which
the absolutist monarchy achieved that the Intendants played an important
role too in supervising and facilitating the expansion of the army. Down
to 1789, for example, they assisted in recruitment, organised the
militia, supervised troop accommodation, controlled a number of other
ancillary services and generally oversaw relations between soldiers and
civilians. From the late 1630s too, a number of Intendants aux armées -
like the Intendants assigned to the provinces, directly responsible to the
crown - were created to supervise the munitions, logistics and financing
of the armies to which they were attached. They checked on all financial transactions, arbitrated in disputes, investigated the dealings of
military suppliers and generally attended to the needs of the army. It
was very much as a result of the activities of the Intendants aux armées
that the most flagrant abuses of the military suppliers and contractors -
'those colossal cheats', in Richelieu's acerbic phrase[9] - were stopped.
The Intendants also had a strategic role vis-à-vis the military high command, for they were briefed to ensure that orders emanating from Paris
were properly observed. Aristocratic commanders regarded it almost
as a derogation of noble status to defer to orders which proceeded from
a civilian bureaucracy in the capital: 'Allez vous faire f.....', one commander told a hapless official brutally, 'avec vos f..... ordres'.[10]
Curbing the aristocratic morgue of generals was not an easy task and
disputes were frequent.

That the bureaucracy was ultimately able to impose its will upon
obstreperous field commanders owed much to the character and abilities
of successive heads of the war department which had sprung up to organise the war effort in the early seventeenth century. First Sublet de
Noyers (from 1637 to 1643), one of Richelieu's favoured créatures, then
Michel Le Tellier (1643 to 1666) followed by his son Louvois (1666 to
1691) were bureaucrats of exceptional administrative gifts. They were
not slow to invoke the authority of ministers and even of the king himself
in order to establish their dominance over the high command. In this
struggle, they were considerably aided by the crown's suppression of a
number of high military posts each of whose incumbents could use his
power, in the words of Louis XIV, to make himself 'more master than
the king himself of the principal strength of the state'.[11] In 1626
Richelieu, acutely aware of the imposing power-base which high military
dignitaries could establish through their control over place and patronage,
had abolished the post of Connétable, formerly supreme commander of

the land forces. At about the same time he also neutralised the
Connétablie's naval equivalents, the Amiral and the Grand général des
Galères. Early in his personal reign, Louis XIV went on to abolish the
similarly prestigious posts of Colonel-général de l'Infanterie and
Colonel-général de la Cavalerie, in 1661 and 1675 respectively.

By the time of Louis XIV's last campaigns, the anarchic, bloody-
minded and entrepreneurial army officer of the time of Richelieu and
Mazarin had given way to an altogether more docile and obedient character. The officer now accounted himself less an autonomous agent and
more - though never entirely - a delegate of royal authority. This trans-
formation was evidently part of the more general process by which the
absolutist state subdued the nobility and defused the threat which they
embodied to political stability. The bureaucracy contributed to the
taming of the noble officer corps. After 1664, for example, the creation
of non-venal posts of high command had the effect of encouraging promotion by merit. The corps might be as thoroughly noble in its social
composition as ever - after all, the monarchy wanted to domesticate the
nobility, not to liquidate them - but a hierarchy of talent now existed
alongside the hierarchy of cash and prestige; and the patronage machines
of regimental commanders had been seriously weakened. Cadet schools
instituted by Louvois encouraged the idea that the status of officer necessitated a degree of instruction. The in-service training in which certain
regiments, especially those of the royal household, specialised, made
them seedbeds of officers for the rest of the army. By the early
eighteenth century too, arrangements were being made for the more
technical military professions such as artillery officers and engineers.
The art of war was on its way to becoming, for the officers, a branch of
a body of learning dispensed by state-controlled agencies. The officer
corps thus illustrated particularly well the absolutist precept that the
nobility could retain their primacy within society at the cost of the re-
pression of their instincts and an acceptance of the framework of social
and political power erected by the state.

5. The Bureaucratisation of the Army: Supplies, Recruitment, Military 'Welfare'

By exerting more rigorous and exacting supervision over the activities of its military subordinates, the state greatly circumscribed the
extent and the effects of decentralisation inherent in the army of
Richelieu's time. It acted further in this direction, morever, by seeking
to extend control over areas of administration formerly in the hands of
colonels, captains and contractors. Not content, in other words, with
overseeing the activities of its servants, the state set out to supplant
them and to build up a less mediated, more direct relationship with the
common soldier. Arms and ammunition, for example, which had pre-
viously been charged for out of wages or on the accounts of commanders,
were gradually standardised and became a state concern. After 1718,

government-sponsored arms factories were producing to order; and after 1727 arms were provided gratis by the state. Uniforms,which strictly speaking had not existed prior to Louis XIV's personal rule, were now generalised at the state's expense. Furthermore, the War Department came to run a proficient system of magazines from which supplies could be drawn. This system, tried out by Le Tellier in the 1640s and perfected by Louvois, did not altogether put an end to armies living off the land. The troops still aimed to live 'at the expense of the enemy'. But the state now supervised and encouraged the 'Contribution System' in preference to indiscriminate plundering; while the magazines supplemented resources appropriated in this way and, during sieges and while the army was on home territory, made the recourse to plunder unnecessary. [12]

Recruitment was a further sphere of military administration in which the central government expanded its role at the expense of troop commanders. Foreign mercenaries, drawn from the poorer regions of Europe such as parts of Ireland, Scotland, Switzerland and Germany, continued to be drawn on; indeed in the eighteenth century they probably comprised a quarter of the army's strength in peace-time and up to a third in time of war. The continuing soundness in the logic behind their use was underlined by Marshal de Saxe:

> 'A German in the army serves us as three soldiers: he
> spares France one, he deprives our enemies of one and
> he serves us as one'. [13]

The practice was now, however, for these mercenaries to serve under French or French-trained officers rather than under their native commanders. By mid eighteenth century, the age of the old mercenary captain was long past; and mercenary troops were subject to the same bureaucratic controls as French troops.

There were other ways too in which the state stimulated recruitment. Indeed it was obliged to make moves in this direction: the old practice of seigneurs recruiting the peasants on their estates proved increasingly unreliable, while the imposition of restraints on plunder effectively dissolved the most potent incentive to recruitment of the early seventeenth-century soldier. A combination of all available methods was necessary to provide the two million men who entered the army in the first two-thirds of the eighteenth century. The enlistment bounty rose faster in this time than the cost of living - a sure sign of the state's difficulties in this sphere. In 1688, a national conscript militia had been formed, members of which were incorporated into the regular forces in time of war. Administrative arrangements were periodically made to facilitate entry into the army of all sorts of social outcasts such as beggars, vagrants, prisoners and orphans. After 1763, moreover, in the interests of greater efficiency and standardisation, the state declared recruitment a royal monopoly and placed the whole system under close bureaucratic scrutiny for the first time.

The government also intervened more and more in the sphere of
military hygiene and welfare which had in the past been almost exclu-
sively the province of unit commanders. From the time of Richelieu
onwards and particularly from the last decades of the seventeenth century, governments spent increasingly large sums on the provision of
regimental medical staff, field hospitals, garrison infirmaries and
chaplaincies. Copious military welfare legislation in the eighteenth
century attested the government's continuing concern in this sphere.
In 1708, for example, 50 royal military hospitals were created and
their number was added to over the course of the century. A hospital
inspectorate was established and more constructive policies towards
hospital and regimental hygiene were adopted. Doctors and surgeons
attached to the army proliferated and were, in the medical profession
as a whole, among the most practically orientated and theoretically
advanced. After 1775, for example, clinical teaching methods - unknown
in the majority of civilian hospitals - were introduced in a number of
military hospitals.

Government military welfare measures were often adduced as
evidence of the benevolent paternalism allegedly characteristic of
Bourbon absolutism. Yet they had a pragmatic edge. The greater
importance of discipline and training in warfare had made the hardened
man-of-war a valuable commodity for which the state was willing to pay
dearly. It thus behoved the government to nurture the object of its
investment. As Richelieu, architect of many of the later welfare policies, had perceived, 'Two thousand soldiers leaving a hospital cured
and in a certain sense broken into their profession' were infinitely pre-
ferable to 'six thousand new recruits'.[14] Moreover, a show of concern
for the welfare of the rank and file bolstered morale as well as
strengthening effectives. Mazarin grasped this point particularly well
in one of his administrative letters:

'I believe we must give priority to everything which is
necessary for hospitals. Besides the fact that charity
requires it, there is nothing which produces a better
effect in armies than that the sick and wounded are
looked after'.[15]

There was a similarly sternly practical intent in the creation in
1670 of the Hôtel des Invalides, a retreat for retired soldiers. Although
the organisers and historians of this institution presented it as an
example of bountiful royal grace and favour, the Invalides was repressive as well as charitable in design. It not only rewarded the meri-
torious veteran; it also aimed to keep off the street the impoverished
and desperate ex-soldier whose activities threatened property and social
stability. Such an idea typified the government's social policy in the
second half of the seventeenth century, which aimed to place social
problem groups within special institutions where they could not harm
society at large. In the same way as, after 1656, the pauper and beggar

would be confined in the hôpital général, or the gypsy (after 1682), the prostitute (after 1684) or the Protestant (after 1685) could find themselves shut away in penal and workhouse-like institutions, so from the last decades of the seventeenth century the ex-soldier, whether disabled or able-bodied, would be likely on completion of his service to find himself placed within the Invalides.

While the Invalides served to insulate the retired soldier from civilian society, the barracks came to perform a similar function for the serving soldier. Barracks rendered largely redundant the violently extractive relationship between soldiers and civilians under the old system of billeting. Within them, the needs of the men could be met by bureaucratic arrangement and not left to private initiative. Significantly, it was a report in 1691 which stated that pillaging by billeted troops in the Maine and Orléanais regions was rendering the local population incapable of paying their taxes which led the government to place its crack troops in barracks. The movement towards barracks which got under way in the next decades was facilitated by the emergence of repressive agencies which rendered the policing function of the regular army less crucial. In the 1690s, police bodies were created in most major towns with powers modelled on those enjoyed since 1667 by the Lieutenant général de police in Paris; and in 1720, the maréchaussée, the para-military mounted police force responsible for the maintenance of law and order in the countryside, was extensively reformed. A royal decree in 1719 stipulated that barracks were to be constructed in towns on all major roads along which troops would be likely to pass. By 1742, over 300 towns contained barracks and by 1775 some 200,000 men were housed in them.

The concentration of troops in barracks also facilitated the instilling of the discipline and self-control which tactical changes had rendered so important on the field of battle. The barrack was a kind of discipline factory. At its most efficient, as with industrial production, greater concentration allowed a much higher degree of control and co-ordination and an inbuilt bias towards technical improvements; at very least the barracks helped keep in check the desertion which was still the running sore of every Ancien Régime army. It encouraged too a regimental esprit de corps. The state poured forth an enormous volume of military regulations in the late seventeenth and eighteenth centuries with the aim of producing, as one manual put it, 'the perfections of the cloister'.[16] Military discipline became in this period not merely a structured and all-encompassing way of life but even a particular mode of bodily comportment: the pace was to be brisk, the head held high, the chest out, the moustache trimmed and shaped, and so on.

The generalisation of disciplinary values among the troops was a development which was popular with the civilian population. Whereas in the early seventeenth century the very mention of troops passing had been enough to provoke a rush for the protection of the woods or of the local

château, with much locking up of wives and daughters, by the late
eighteenth century, in contrast, civilians were as likely to turn up and
cheer as the gallant soldiery marched by with their bright uniforms to
the regular beat of the drum and the sound of military music. This
greater acceptance of - even fondness for - the common soldier owed
much also to the fact that, unlike the previous century, the eighteenth
century saw very little fighting or civil strife on French soil. This,
along with barracks, the Invalides, the imposition of discipline and the
growth of state controls over military subsistence distanced the army
physically from the rest of society.

6. The Lot of the Common Soldier

If, as a result of this constellation of changes, the army was
infinitely more professional than before, and much less feared and
hated by the civilian population, the soldiers themselves did not necessarily approve of the resultant changes in their life-style. The reforms
aimed to achieve efficiency, not well-being; they treated the men as un-
reasoning objects of administration rather than as human beings with
flesh and blood under their military uniforms.

One of military life's traditional compensations upon which military regulations now frowned, for example, was sex. Camp-following
prostitutes had been an accepted part of the baggage-train of every
European army in the early seventeenth century, when military theo-
rists calculated that they should be allowed to flourish at the rate of
four to every hundred men. By the end of the century, however, in
France as elsewhere in Europe, 'we find' (to use the clipped Germanic
English of historian Fritz Redlich) 'a policy of restricting soldiers'
copulations'.[17] A series of laws passed between 1684 and 1687, aimed
apparently both to arrest the spread of syphilis among the troops and to
make them more willing to risk death in battle by giving them less to
live for, stipulated that any prostitute found within two leagues of a military camp was to have her nose and ears split. Military regulations at
about the same time actively discouraged the marriage of troops. More
populationist military policies towards the end of the eighteenth century
caused a relaxation of the ban on marriage. Prostitutes were still
frowned on however - by the authorities at least. If the laws of 1684
and 1687 were no longer applied in all their grisly detail, new regulations in 1768 stated that any prostitute found consorting with the troops
should be imprisoned. In 1781, any soldier who caught venereal disease
more than three (!) times was obliged to spend an extra two years service within the army.

The example of sex is a good illustration of the fact that the professionalisation of the army did not necessarily improve the perceived
well-being of the common soldier. True, soldiers were now relatively
protected from being swindled by their commanders, and the worst

excesses of the military suppliers had also been checked. True, too, wages were now paid with greater regularity and exactitude. Nevertheless, all was far from rosy. The state's financial position never permitted it to do without private contractors, and inefficiency and corruption could still reappear in the supply services, especially when the system was strained by war-time conditions. If wages rose over the course of the century, prices rose faster. With the higher echelons of command fiercely competed for by nobles and bourgeois, chances of promotion must have remained slim. Moreover, although more officers were found urging humane treatment of their men, the aura of success attaching to Frederick the Great's Prussian army meant that the imported codes of discipline were Spartan at best, Draconian at worst.

Despite the state's elaboration of wide-ranging ancillary and welfare services, therefore, the soldier's lot was still a far from happy one. His living conditions were often little short of abysmal. If uniforms were now issued free of charge, it was widely acknowledged that they were more suited to the parade-ground than the battlefield or military camp. Moreover, in war-time they were frequently in short supply. The old military diseases - apart from plague - were still rife. Indeed, there is a strong case for arguing that the move into barracks made the troops more susceptible than before to 'crowd diseases' such as typhus, typhoid fever and dysentery. Certainly, conditions in barracks could be most insanitary. The constructions were often jerry-built and were insufficiently heated or ventilated; overcrowding was always a problem; and even at the best of times the men slept two to a bed. Life on campaign continued to be brimful of miseries and privations. 'Once the rainy season has arrived', commented Marshal de Saxe of the general conditions of the common soldier, 'his head is seldom dry. As for his feet, it cannot be doubted that his stockings, shoes and feet all rot together'.[18] Hospital care for the ailing was unimpressive, especially in time of war. Health care was often hardest hit by cash shortages and the corruption of military suppliers. The Marquis de Feuquières commented following the War of Austrian Succession, for example, that

'The roguery committed in the hospitals is limitless...
Greed for profit induces the entrepreneurs to act beyond
all consideration of humanity'.[19]

So deep-dyed were corruption and abuse in the military hospitals, indeed, that regulations on the eve of the Revolution envisaged the total closure of the vast majority and their replacement by regimental infirmaries which would, it was hoped, prove less of a health risk than the old hospitals.

The now accepted restrictions on plunder also severely reduced a component of the soldier's income which had allowed his seventeenth-century forebear a chance of emerging from his army days with money in his pocket. From the ranks, greater state control over the

'Contribution System', for example, must have seemed tantamount to forcible expropriation. Denied the opportunity of engaging in the petty entrepreneurial activities of appropriation and disposal of loot, and more dependent than before on his wage, the soldier had become proletarianised. He was more likely to end his soldiering days destitute. The economy found it difficult to absorb soldiers especially in the mass demobilisations following the end of a war when up to 100,000 men might suddenly be thrown onto the labour market. It was symptomatic of the problem for social order which the ex-soldier comprised that the main bouts of government legislation against criminal vagrancy occurred in the years following the end of major wars: 1719, 1720 and 1724 after the demobilisations of 1717 and 1718; 1750, after the War of Austrian Succession (1740-1748); and 1764 and 1767 after the Seven Years' War (1756-1763). Aware of the social threat that the demobilised soldier represented, conscious of welfare provisions as a possible incentive to recruitment and somewhat influenced too by the voguish philanthropy current towards the end of the Ancien Régime, the state turned its mind to the care of the retiring soldier. The Order of Saint Louis, established in 1693, provided pensions for valorous retired officers; the Invalides was expanded so that by the end of the Ancien Régime its numbers exceeded 30,000 men; and soldiers with very long terms of service were, from the 1760s onwards, awarded a pension as of right. As the prelude to the French Revolution was to reveal, however, all this was to a certain extent only papering over widening cracks.

7. The Aftermath of the Seven Years' War: Reforms and Tensions

Military welfare measures illustrate the wish of the monarchy to use every means at hand to build and maintain a large army of well-disciplined career professionals. Yet the proof of the pudding lies in the eating: the miseries of the everyday life of the common soldier highlighted the insufficiences of the state's commitment in this sphere. Such failings remained relatively masked as long as the French kept their reputation as having the most formidable army in Europe. The stunning military defeats which they endured at the hands of Prussia in the Seven Years' War, however, provided a rude and unwelcome shock to a complacent military establishment. Besides contributing to the ruination of the state's finances under the pressure of colossal military expenditure, the war thus called into question if not the rationale at least the effectiveness of the state's measures to achieve the full professionalisation of its army. There followed a spate of reforms aimed at rectifying matters by increased state control. In the darkening social and political atmosphere of the final decades of the Ancien Régime, however, with state bankruptcy threatening on the horizon, attempts to ensure the further professionalisation of the army only brought to the surface of military life a host of complexes, strains and resentments whose consequences were to transcend the inner workings of the military machine.

Much of the state's attention was now focussed on streamlining the officer corps. Though far more ready to accept the structures of discipline and training imposed by the state than their pre-Fronde ancestors, most nobles still aspired to maintain their corps - which the Seven Years' War had nevertheless revealed as riddled with privilege, private fiefs and petty vanities - as a preeminently noble preserve. Over-zealous reform in this sphere touched many raw nerves. The phasing out of the evidently unprofessional practice of purchase of commissions after 1776, for example, aroused the hostility of potential buyers. Preference now given to nobles who had been presented at court profoundly irritated ambitious commoners and country gentry who aspired to posts of high command. Commoners and the newly-ennobled were also upset by the notorious Ségur ordinance of 1781. This regulation which attempted to restrict entry to the officer corps to individuals with four generations of nobility in their families typified the thinking behind much of the reform movement which was that, although the occasional gifted commoner might make a good officer, it was above all noble stock which produced the required military virtues. All officers, whether nobles or not, were, however, likely to be dismayed by government measures which, in the interests of economy, abolished many posts and even disbanded companies. The state was evidently finding it increasingly difficult to afford a large standing army. From the point of view of the officers, however, cheeseparing of this sort reduced career prospects. Finally, many officers were to feel that the government's attack in the late 1780s on the fiscal privileges of the class from which most derived was unconstitutional and placed them outside their oath of loyalty. The common front which many made, between 1786 and 1788, with their noble confrères in the Assembly of Notables, the Parlements and the Assembly of the Clergy revealed the failure of the apparent professionalisation of the army officer corps over the course of the seventeenth and eighteenth centuries to expunge basic class solidarities.

The picture was much the same at the other end of the social spectrum. For the army rank and file, the reforms of the last decades of the Ancien Régime consisted in a further attempt to improve efficiency rather than living conditions. The new Prussian-style disciplinary code was particularly deeply hated. The deterioration of morale among officers may also, in turn, have affected the common soldiers. In addition, the troops came to resent the way in which, at the height of the social and economic crisis of the late 1780s, they were used as a policing agency to quell grain riots and other disturbances. This policy in fact probably intensified the sympathy which the soldiers felt for the peasantry and the urban labouring classes, from whose ranks they were themselves drawn. Certainly by early 1789 there were substantial portions of the army on whose obedience the king could no longer count. It was highly appropriate that, on 14 July 1789, the fall of the Bastille, supreme symbol of the naked coercive power of French absolutism, should be engineered by dissident soldiers.

By the end of the Ancien Régime, the structural limits of the
policies of centralised state control over military institutions and the
insulation of the army from the rest of society were seemingly being
reached. The standing army forged in the wake of the Military Revolution had, it is true, permitted successive Bourbon rulers to sustain
a permanent challenge to European hegemony. This was only achieved,
however, at the cost of financial strains which tore the state asunder in
the 1780s. Moreover, dependence on the nobility - one, if not the,
major bulwark of absolutist rule - for the staffing of the officer corps
imposed certain limitations on the professionalisation and centralisation which were the state's constant aim. The perceived need to revit-
alise the officer corps after the disasters of the Seven Years' War
meant the monarchy overstepping the long-drawn and tacitly-agreed
line dividing state interest from noble privilege. The involvement of
the officer corps - and, in a different but no less important way, the
rank and file - in the outbreak of the Revolution showed that, despite
the instilling of disciplinary and professional values, soldiers were
not the mindless automata which the military machine required but
self-interested and reasoning members of a wider community. The
events of the Revolutionary decade were to underline this fact even
more spectacularly. In wider perspective too, the secure position of
military institutions at the heart of the absolutist state helped produce
a fatal unevenness in the development of the French armed forces. In
particular the failure to build up a strong navy cost the French dear.
Just as the unimpressive performances of the regular troops in the
Seven Years' War revealed deficiencies in the army's vaunted
'professionalism', so too overseas losses in the same war showed the
inability of an army alone to achieve a sound basis for international
dominance in the expanding mercantile economy. By the late eighteenth
century, the French recipe for military strength and state power which,
since the mid seventeenth century other states had found so attractive,
was made to seem outmoded by another, more naval, more mercantile
power: England.

NOTES

1. For the historiographical debate on the Military Revolution, see the Introduction to this volume.

2. For a table of increases in army size, G. Parker, 'The "Military Revolution", 1560-1660 - a myth?', Journal of Modern History (1976), p.206. For France, cf. the additional materials in G. d'Avenel, Richelieu et la monarchie absolue (4 vols., Paris, 1884-1890), pp.42-43; and A. Babeau, La Vie militaire sous l'Ancien Régime (2 vols., 1889-1890), i, p.14 n.

3. R. Mandrou, Louis XIV en son temps, 1661-1715 (Paris, 1973), p.229.

4. Cited in G. d'Avenel, op. cit., iii, p.148.

5. D'Avenel, op. cit., iii, p.99.

6. Richelieu, Testament politique, critical edition edited by L. André (Paris, 1947), p.480.

7. Cited by X. Auduoin, Histoire de l'administration de la guerre, (Paris, 1811), p.232.

8. W. O. Doyle, The Old European Order, 1660-1800 (Oxford, 1978), p.253.

9. D'Avenel, op. cit., p.133.

10. Ibid, p.56.

11. Cited in M. Marion, Dictionnaire des institutions de la France aux XVIIe. siècle (Paris, reprint, 1968), p.111.

12. See the discussion of this important aspect of military administration in M. van Creveld, Supplying War: logistics from Wallenstein to Patton (Cambridge, 1977), pp.23-26.

13. Cited in A. Corvisier, L'Armée française de la fin du XVIIe. siècle au ministère de Choiseul. Le soldat (2 vols., Paris, 1964), i, p.260.

14. Cited in A. Cabanès, Chirurgiens et blessés à travers l'histoire: des origines à la Croix-rouge (Paris, 1912), p.167 n.

15. Cited in J. Des Cilleuls, 'Le Service de santé en campagne aux armées de l'Ancien Régime', Revue historique de l'Armée (1950), p.7.

16. Boussanelle, cited in M. Foucault, Discipline and Punish. The Birth of the Prison, English translation (Harmondsworth, 1979), p.150.

17. F. Redlich, The German Military Enterpriser and his Work-force. A Study in European economic and social history (2 vols., Wiesbaden, 1964), p.208.

18. Ibid, p.226.

19. Cited in A. Cabanès, op. cit., p.256.

3. The Foundations of British Naval Power

MICHAEL DUFFY

1. The initial stage of naval expansion

The Military Revolution on land was paralleled by a simultaneous revolution at sea which saw its greatest development in the growth of the British Royal Navy. In 1514, at the end of his first war with France, Henry VIII was able to send to sea 23 ships of the Royal Navy and 36 hired merchant vessels, the whole manned by 4,429 men. Throughout the sixteenth century the Tudor Royal Navy rarely mustered more than thirty ships. Even in England's year of crisis, 1588, there were only 34 Crown ships and only 197 ships altogether taken into royal pay against the Spanish Armada - the other 163 were either volunteered by private individuals and groups or levied by the Crown together with a quota of men from each port. It was a far cry from the situation just over two centuries later at the end of Great Britain's last war with France, when the Royal Navy was maintaining over 1,000 purpose-built Crown warships manned by 130,000 men.

There were two reasons for this earlier state of affairs. Firstly, the Crown lacked the financial capacity to build and maintain a large Royal Navy. The highest numbers attained in the sixteenth century were Henry VIII's 58 ships of 1546, built on the proceeds of the Dissolution of the Monasteries, but which could not be continued when this source dried up. Secondly it was both cheaper and also compatible with the needs of contemporary naval warfare to hire armed merchant vessels and private warships in times of emergency. The specialist warship was still the exception rather than the norm and in the melée tactics of the day it was always possible for any ship to find another of equal size to fight, so that the private resources of its subjects could always supplement the nucleus of the Royal Navy whenever the Crown needed to expand its naval force. The exchange was mutual in that Elizabeth not infrequently let out ships of the Royal Navy to private individuals for trading and raiding.

In consequence the build-up of English naval strength in the late sixteenth century was due less to the growth of the Royal Navy than to the growth in numbers of private armed ships as individuals or groups sought to take advantage of the chance of booty in the Spanish Empire during the long war with Spain. Private finance, manpower and enterprise were the main constituents of the armed cutting-edge of English naval power and English empire which the Crown encouraged because it lacked the money to act in this sphere. Many of the great trading or colonising companies of the second half of the sixteenth and early seventeenth centuries were formed to provide capital not just to trade but to fight: indeed they had to fight to get to their markets, to break the monopoly of markets or colonies of the Spanish, the Portuguese and later the Dutch, and to fend off interlopers trying to seize what they had won. For its expedition to the Orient in 1601 to break the Portuguese spice monopoly, the East India Company bought the most powerful private English warship afloat - the 600 ton, 36 gun Red Dragon - which stood comparison with all but the few largest ships in the Royal Navy.

As late as 1625-8 the Crown was still relying predominantly on hiring private ships and manpower when it wished to increase its fleet for major operations (Table A).

Table A

Composition of British fleets 1625-28

	Royal warships	Merchant ships
Cadiz expedition 1625	12	73
1st La Rochelle expedition 1627	14	82
2nd La Rochelle expedition 1628	29	31

Source: Oppenheim, Administration of the Royal Navy p.251

By this time, however, pressures were mounting for the Royal Navy to be increased and improved. Warship design was now clearly diverging from that of merchantmen as considerations of speed and gunnery capacity became more important (Table B). The increase in merchant shipping led to demands for naval protection in the Channel and western approaches whither Barbary corsairs, Dunkirk privateers and pirates were being attracted by the prospect of booty. The major difficulty in the way of increasing the Royal Navy however again became apparent when Charles I sought money for warship building in 1634. The constitutional controversy over Ship Money led to it being abolished by Parliament in 1641, and even before that its yield had begun to dry up in 1638 as the nation started to baulk at Charles's other policies. War with the Scots and constitutional conflict with Parliament left the Crown without money to continue its new policy of naval armament, and the Royal fleet, after a decade of being starved of food, clothing and pay because of the Crown's financial shortcomings, readily joined the Parliamentary cause in the Civil War.

Table B

The increase in warship size and strength 1561-1786

(a) The biggest warships (Ships Royal, later First Rates)

	Built	Tons	Guns	Men
Triumph	1561	955	40-45	500
Prince Royal	1610	1200	55	
Sovereign of the Seas	1637	1522	100-105	
Britannia	1682	1708	100	780
Britannia	1762	2091	100	850

(b) Average strong warships (Great Ships, later Third Rates)

	Built	Tons	Guns	Men
Revenge	1577	450	30-34	
Vanguard	1630 (rebuilt)	750	40	4-500
Lyme	1654	1025	52	
Ipswich	1694	1049	70	450
Elephant	1786	1644	74	600

Sources: Oppenheim, Administration of the Royal Navy, p. 120, 124, 202, 255, 334-5; Ehrman, Navy in the War of William III, p. 626; Merriman (ed.), Queen Anne's Navy, p. 336; Victoria Co. History of Hampshire, Vol. 5 p. 391, 398.

2. The build-up of the Royal Navy

The navy grew through three stages during the second half of the seventeenth century. The first and formative period was that of the Republic. During the Civil War by means of the assessments, the excise and particularly the sale of sequestered royalist estates, Parliament at last produced a revenue capable of building and of temporarily sustaining a large government-owned navy (the ability of the Republic to sustain this navy diminished rapidly as it ran out of land to sell at the end of the 1650s). The means were thus available, over the short-term at least, and the need had increased too, as the commercial ravages of the Royalists were added to those of other privateers and corsairs, and as the Republic became involved first in a war with Holland, the strongest naval and commercial power of the day, and then in a war with Spain. The hard-fought battles of the Dutch war revealed shortcomings in hiring armed merchant ships under their own captains - the latter would not follow orders and were shy of risking damage to their ships in battle. Blake, one of the Republic's Generals-at-Sea, urged that in future no more than two-fifths of the fleet should be composed of private ships. In practise, moreover, tactical and gunnery developments were rapidly imposing a limitation on their use as the need became recognized for a professional navy in purpose-built ships: this first Dutch war saw the establishment of the first statutory code of naval discipline (The Articles of War) and the first official set of Fighting Instructions, both in 1653.

In consequence the latter part of the Civil War and the period of the Republic saw an unprecedented period of naval building, supplemented by prizes taken from the Dutch and Spanish. This initial stage of the build-up of the navy was primarily of smaller craft. If the system of rating ships according to guns as developed later in the century is transposed on the figures given by Oppenheim this trend becomes apparent in Table C.

Table C

The growth of the navy 1646-59

	Ships built	Ships captured and commissioned	Grand Total
1st Rate (96-100 guns)	0	0	0
2nd Rate (80-90 guns)	1	0	1
3rd Rate (60-74 guns)	7*	0	7
4th Rate (40-54 guns)	35	3	38
5th Rate (28-38 guns)	20	32	52
6th Rate (16-26 guns)	20	31	51
Others	23	45	68
	106	111	217

* includes one 56-gun ship

Source: Oppenheim, Administration of the Navy, pp.255, 330-7. Nine ships captured at unspecified dates during the Civil War have been omitted. N.B. This table can only be an approximation for comparison with later periods since the Republic rated ships according to crew-size and many of the captured vessels were not purpose-built warships but armed merchantmen which were sold as soon as they were not needed.

Smaller warships were better suited to the need for fast, shallow-draught vessels to chase the speedy Dunkirkers and to get inshore amongst the shallows of the coasts of Holland and Flanders. By 1660 the navy was large in ships but because they were mostly 4th rate and below, it was still small in manpower (Table N).

The second stage of the naval build-up came under Charles II and James II when although the Royal Navy did not increase greatly in number of ships, it did expand markedly in manpower. This reflects a character-change towards larger ships. Such a development was the natural result of the new tactical formation evolved by the Commonwealth Navy in the first Dutch war (1652-4) and which was then imitated by other states. In the sixteenth century the English had been foremost in developing gunnery tactics at sea (partly due to the excellent ordnance produced in the Weald of Kent) in preference to the old practice of boarding or the new alternative of fireships. This preference was again noted as peculiar to the English navy by observers in the Dutch wars of the third quarter of the seventeenth century. Just as on land the growing use of firepower led to a reversion to linear formations so as to maximise the ability to get as many guns into action at once and thus hit as hard as possible, so at sea the English turned to line-of-battle tactics, forming a long line of destructive gun batteries, a practice confirmed by the Duke of York's Additional Fighting Instructions of 1665 and 1673. Once the tactic had been adopted the next step was to increase the power of these gun batteries and in consequence warships increased decisively in size and gunpower (Table B). Greater numbers of the 1st-3rd rates were built. In 1660 there were only three 1st and 2nd rates and perhaps seven of the 3rd, but between 1663-75 thirteen 1st and 2nd rates and twelve 3rds were built for the Royal Navy. Indeed in the 1660s and 70s a naval arms race developed as the English, French and Dutch built up their bigger ships, now designated ships of the line (of battle), in order to secure naval supremacy. In 1677 Parliament, frightened at the growth of French naval power, voted £600,000 for building 30 ships of the 1st -3rd rates. By 1689 the strength of the Royal Navy was distributed as in Table D.

Table D

Composition of the Royal Navy 1689

Rates	1st	2nd	3rd	4th	5th	6th	Others	Total
	9	11	39	41	2	6	65	173

Source: Ehrman, Navy in the War of William III, p.4

In fact this up-rating of the composition of the navy probably went too far, for in the third stage of the naval build-up, during the war of 1689-97, the expansion of the top rates was halted. They were too expensive in manpower and useless for anything except fleet actions.

Nor were they good sailors and could only be kept at sea during the
milder summer months. The tendency was therefore to rely more on
3rd and 4th rates for battle fleets. Moreover as the French abandoned
seeking fleet actions and turned increasingly to commerce raiding, so
the need for the top rates diminished still further while the need for
greater numbers of smaller craft grew. Expansion therefore went back
to the lower rates and lesser vessels and the composition of the Royal
Navy was now established more or less for the whole future period of
British naval ascendancy (Table E, Table F).

Table E

British naval shipbuilding 1660-1697

Rates	1st	2nd	3rd	4th	5th	6th	Others	Total
(a) ships built 1660-88	10	14	32	15	7	7	22	107
(b) 1689-97								
ships built	-	3	20	35	25	20	52	155
rebuilt	3	1	2	3	3	-	-	12
bought	-	-	-	1	5	2	38	46
	3	4	22	39	33	22	90	213

Sources: Coleman, 'Stuart Dockyards', p.137; Ehrman, Navy in the
War of William III, p.630-1.

Table F

Composition of the Royal Navy 1697

Rates	1st	2nd	3rd	4th	5th	6th	Others	Total
	6	13	43	56	42	40	123	323

Source: Ehrman, Navy in the War of William III, p.620.

Throughout the eighteenth century the battlefleet of 1st-4th rate
ships - the ships of line - stabilized at between 110-130 ships. In
mid-century there was an improvement when Lord Anson as head of the
Admiralty revised the ratings so as to strengthen the line of battle and
the 74-gun warship became the basic British battleship (Table G cf.
the ratings in Table C).

At the same time the constant growth of British commerce and
empire requiring protection from enemy raiders led to a continual
expansion of the lesser-rated frigates and of ship-and brig-sloops
(Table H shows the trend in peacetime. Many more were built in war
and sold or broken up in peace).

Table G

The re-rating of warships in the middle of the eighteenth century

Rates	1st	2nd	3rd	4th	5th	6th	sloops
Guns	100-120	90-98	64-80	50-60*	32-44	20-28	14-18

* Only 60 gun 4th rates were to be included in the line of battle.

Source: William James, The Naval History of Great Britain (London, 1837), Vol.1, Appendix Table No.1.

Table H

The increase in numbers of 5th and 6th rates in the Royal Navy

1714	1751	1793
66	78	114

Sources: Merriman, Queen Anne's Navy, p.363; Baugh, British Naval Administration, p.530; James, Naval History, I, Appendix Table No.1. N.B. From James's figures for 1 Jan. 1793 only ships in commission or 'in ordinary' have been included; 6 being built and 17 stationary harbour-ships are omitted.

In contrast therefore to the Military Revolution on land, where established armies tended to reach a maximum size during the War of the Spanish Succession at the beginning of the eighteenth century and then levelled out or even declined thereafter, and in contrast to its leading naval rivals who peaked in the 1690s and then fell away abruptly, the Royal Navy continued to expand (Table N), an expansion both caused by and sustained by Britain's constantly expanding sea-borne commerce.

In other ways also the Military Revolution at sea differed from that on land. There was a continuing place for private enterprise in sea-warfare alongside the professional navies. The exploitation of economic warfare at sea, with its opportunities of profit for commerce-raiders, led to the arming of private vessels as privateers with government sanction. It also induced the larger long-distance merchantmen to continue to arm themselves for their own protection. Ships of the Levant Company and the Royal African Company mounted up to 24-30 guns in wartime, larger East India Company ships carried even more and were so strong that as late as 1795 the Royal Navy met a temporary warship shortage by buying East Indiamen. The East India Company even kept its own private navy based on Bombay which at the beginning of the nineteenth century numbered 2 frigates, 3 ship-sloops and 14 brig-sloops. Although private enterprise no longer had a place in the line of battle, it still had a very significant lesser rôle to play.

Lastly, a standing navy was not the same as a standing army. Fleets were too expensive in men and material to remain mobilized in peacetime. During the Dutch wars they were even laid up and their crews paid off during the winter months. This however led to the national humiliation of the Dutch surprising and destroying part of the unmanned fleet in the Medway in 1667, and from the end of the century the fleet was kept in a state of more or less continual readiness in wartime. When peace came however it was still the practice to disarm most of the fleet, to lay up the big battleships on a repair and maintenance basis, and to sell off many of the less durable smaller craft which could quickly be replaced by new shipbuilding in the event of a future war. Only a small force of 15-30 battleships and of frigates was maintained for emergencies and for commerce protection overseas, and these had diminished crews. Otherwise officers were put on half-pay and the men paid off to return to the merchant marine (since their basic drill was seamanship which could be learnt in private employ there was less need to retain them than in the armies whose specialized drill could only be learnt on the parade-ground). The Royal Navy could thus be 76,000 strong in 1763 and only 17,500 strong in the following year of peace. What was 'standing' about a standing navy in peacetime was a small active force, the officers on half-pay, the bulk of the battleships laid up 'in ordinary', and the dockyard facilities which, because they were still needed to maintain the battleships, were probably only reduced by about a third of their manpower in peacetime. The system caused problems in mobilization at the start of a war, but its economic advantages for Britain, which did not have to maintain a large standing army, were considerable. In contrast to the continental powers the largest part of its armed forces could be redeployed to foster the economy in peacetime rather than be kept on the economically sterile parade ground.

3. Problems in creating a large Royal Navy: shipbuilding and maintenance

Naval supremacy does not simply exist. It has to be created and maintained. The effort to do so profoundly altered the extent of British government, the national finances, and foreign policy. It influenced the national economy and inevitably affected society as well. To create naval power involved the solution by experiment of four basic problems: how to find the ships; how to find the men to man them; how to administer and maintain the Navy thus created; and how to defeat the enemy at sea (the last only capable of resolution after the first three). On their solution Britain's great-power position ultimately depended.

Finding the ships itself involved the resolution of two problems: the creation of facilities to build and maintain ships and the finding of the necessary raw materials for ship construction. The underpinning of naval construction was the growth of private ship-building

through the growth of the coal trade between Durham and London in
the mid-sixteenth century, the development of trade with Russia, the
Baltic and the Mediterranean and the exploitation of the Newfoundland
and Icelandic fisheries in the late sixteenth century, and most decisively
the development of a great overseas trade with the Caribbean, North
America and India in the 'commercial revolution' of the seventeenth
century. This trade was preserved for English shipping by the
Navigation Act of 1651, confirmed and strengthened in 1660 and
defended in the Dutch wars. Thereafter, protected by the law and the
growing Royal Navy, English merchant tonnage expanded rapidly
(Table I) and sustained a growing private shipbuilding industry which
provided an essential reserve of trained ship-builders and of shipbuilding facilities to supplement the government's own shipbuilding
efforts in wartime.

Table I

The growth of English shipping tonnage

1572	50,000	1751	421,000
1629	115,000	1764	523,000
1686	340,000	1775	608,000
1702	323,000	1786	752,000

Source: Davis, Rise of the English Shipping Industry,
p.27.
These figures are for English shipping only.
A 1792 report put the total tonnage of Britain
and its empire at 1,540,000 tons, (Lloyd,
The English Seaman, p.285-6). For Royal
Naval tonnage see Table N.

Most battleships, and in particular all 1st and 2nd rates, were
built in the royal dockyards, partly because private yards lacked the
facilities and expertise to build the biggest warships, but more to ensure
a consistent and controlled standard of construction. Above all royal
dockyards met the fleet's needs for frequent large-scale docking for
repair and maintenance which was beyond the resources of private
yards. Yet between 1650 and 1690 Republic and Monarchy alike concentrated what money they had into building up the fleet rather than
building up the dockyard resources to sustain it. Only three dry-docks
were added during the expansion between 1650 and 1684 for a fleet that
had more than trebled in numbers and increased vastly more in ship
size. It was fortunate - indeed necessary - that each of the Dutch wars
was of such short duration because the royal dockyards could not have
sustained the fleet for a prolonged struggle.

The obstacle was probably lack of money. In the 1680s and '90s
however there was a considerable improvement in Crown finances

which enabled both the fleet and the necessary dockyard facilities for its maintenance to be built up. Increasing trade swelled the income from customs and excise while accord on internal and foreign policy between Crown and Parliament in the early 1690s produced major advances in a lucrative land tax and a Parliament-backed system of government borrowing. In the event the delay in dockyard expansion proved fortunate because money became available just at the moment when an entire refocussing of facilities became necessary. Hitherto except for a double dry-dock built at Portsmouth in 1659, the focus of the naval yards had been on the Thames which was the centre of national shipbuilding and supply. This system suited a Dutch war and the initial expansion when money became available in 1684-5 was the addition of two more dry-docks at Chatham. However in 1689 England embarked on a war with France and at once there was a need for dock-yard facilities to back operations in the Channel and western approaches. Between 1690 and 1704 two new dry-docks and two basins were added at Portsmouth, whose dockyard workforce supplanted Chatham's by 1697 as the largest in the country, and between 1690 and 1698 an entirely new dockyard with a basin and large dry-dock was built at Plymouth.

Further docks were added at the two Channel yards in the eighteenth century as the French wars continued, and a new pattern emerged whereby the old Thames and Medway yards, Deptford, Wool-wich and Chatham, served as centres for provisioning, shipbuilding and major repairs, while Sheerness (built at the mouth of the Medway during the third Dutch war for North Sea operations), Portsmouth (for the Channel fleet and all overseas expeditions) and Plymouth (for squadrons guarding the Western approaches) were yards for operational repairs and equipment. There were also supply and cleaning bases at Harwich and at Kinsale on the southern coast of Ireland, and during the eighteenth century there also developed a network of overseas bases and dockyards which greatly extended the durability of British seapower in distant waters: at Gibralter and Port Mahon (Minorca) for the Mediterranean and the blockade of Cadiz in wars with Spain; at Port Royal (Jamaica) and English Harbour (Antigua) for the Caribbean; and at Boston and later Halifax (Nova Scotia) for North America. There was however a basic lack of dry-dock facilities for major repairs overseas.

The expansion both of the navy and of the number and size of the royal dockyards greatly increased the extent of government involvement in the economy. John Ehrman has described the navy in 1688 as 'the most comprehensive, and in some respects the largest industry in the country'. [1] The government was the biggest single builder of ships and the biggest single purchaser of ships built in private yards. The navy's dominance in marine construction and repair can be estimated from a shipwrights' petition to the Board of Trade in the depression year of 1724 which claimed that there were less than a thousand shipwrights employed in private shipbuilding in Britain, while at their nadir

of employment for the century in the following year the naval dockyards had 1,564 shipwrights on their books.[2]

The dockyards made the government one of the country's major
single employers of civilian labour (Table J).

Table J

The dockyard labour-force in 1711 and 1772

	1711	1772
Deptford	1083	939
Woolwich	926	868
Chatham	1287	1353
Sheerness	234	439
Portsmouth	2001	2228
Plymouth	717	2033
Harwich	88	-
Kinsale	33	?
	6369	8060

Sources: Merriman, Queen Anne's Navy, p.373;
V.C.H. Kent, Vol.2 p.378. 1711 was a war
year and 1772 one of peace.

Relations with such a concentrated and skilled workforce were
never easy and were not helped by the government's parsimony in the
wages it offered and its delays in paying them. At times in the 1689-97
and 1756-63 wars pay was up to fifteen months in arrears. A study of
industrial relations in the dockyards in the eighteenth century would
reveal a prototype for many of the forms of class-struggle characteristic of later centuries (organised strikes, workings to rule etc.), a
major difference being that later employers could not withdraw their
workers' protections and have them pressed into the navy as the
Admiralty did to break a strike of smiths at the Thames and Medway
yards in 1744. Indeed the unattractiveness of the employment forced
the government to impress shipwrights into its dockyards in times of
greatest shortage in the seventeenth and early eighteenth centuries.
Subsequently expedients were devised to improve conditions[3], but the
price the navy always had to pay was widespread corruption and
wastage in its yards as its employees sought to supplement their pay
in whatever way they could. It was claimed at one prosecution in 1801
that £500,000 a year was embezzled at the dockyards. It was fortunate
that the country had the financial capacity to sustain such wastage and
still equip its fleets.[4]

The expansion of private shipbuilding and the growth of the naval dockyards meant that there was no question as before of Britain having the necessary facilities to build and maintain as many warships as it needed provided it could obtain the materials to build them. The effort to secure these materials both for the navy and for the merchant marine on which naval strength so much depended, drew the government even further into intervention in the economy and, still more, constituted an entire imperial and foreign policy in itself.

The complexities of this aspect of the shipbuilding problem are best illustrated by a list of the essential requirements for warship construction and their sources (Table K).

Table K

Origins of shipbuilding materials and naval stores.

Material	Use	Source
Timber	Hull-frames	Oak, preferably Sussex oak.
"	Planking	Baltic oak, English elm for below the waterline.
"	Mainmasts, main yards, bowsprits.	Great pines from the Baltic, New England and Canada.
"	Middling masts	Pines from the Ukraine obtained through Riga and the Baltic ports.
"	Lesser masts and yards	Young spruce from Norway.
Iron	Anchors, nails, cannon, shot	Spain (particularly for anchors), Sweden, England.
Canvas	Sails	France, Holland, Germany (via Hamburg), eventually England.
Hemp	Ropemaking	Russia, Eastern Baltic, small amounts from England and Ireland.
Tar and pitch	Ropemaking, waterproofing	Sweden, southern colonies of British North America.

For both timber and naval stores Britain, like the other western European naval powers, remained largely dependent on the Baltic and this dictated the direction of British foreign policy in that area. It

strove perpetually to maintain an open door from the Baltic and
within the shores of that sea Britain sought a balance of power to
prevent any Baltic state gaining a monopoly of these precious materials.
Between 1658 and 1813 there were some 20 naval expeditions to the
Baltic for this purpose. The policy also had a corollary in that, while
seeking to ensure its own naval supplies, Britain sought equally to
starve its enemies of them, and in wartime this produced a constant
wrangle with neutrals over what cargoes were immune from seizure.
In 1780 and again in 1801 the Baltic powers leagued together in an Armed
Neutrality against British methods. In the latter case the navy attacked
the Danish fleet at Copenhagen to break the combination. In 1807 it
bombarded neutral Copenhagen again to forestall any attempt by the
French to seize the Danish fleet and shut the Sound. By fair means or
foul the government, backed by naval coercion, kept the supplies of
Baltic shipbuilding material coming through.

Wherever possible the government sought to break the Baltic
stranglehold and gain at the same time a self-sufficiency. It had a
major advantage over its rivals in its possession of the virgin forests
of North America whose giant pinus strobus could provide mainmasts
up to 40 ins. in diameter whereas Baltic pines were restricted to 27 ins.
maximum. A policy initiated in the Massachusetts Charter of 1691
and extended by Acts of 1722 and 1728 to all colonies from New Jersey
northwards reserved all trees over 24 ins. diameter for the navy. The
advantage the navy secured from this supply was revealed when it
dried up during the American War of Independence and several
squadrons with worn out masts or inferior composite masts were
dismasted in storms and rendered unoperational. Thereafter the navy
developed Canadian New Brunswick for its needs. All the hull timber
was originally supplied in Britain itself, but this was a diminishing
asset. Elizabeth and the early Stuarts sold off large areas of the royal
forests in their need for ready money. The Republic's shipbuilding
was not matched by compensatory replanting. Despite Acts regulating
felling and replanting in certain royal forests (1668, 1698), Acts
against deforestation (1714, 1720), and propagandist works such as
John Evelyn's Sylva of 1664, private owners were always tempted to
cash in on their woodlands in the eighteenth century before their oaks
reached the size the navy needed for hull frames. From the 1680s the
navy was looking to the Baltic for much of its oak planking, and though
the supply of home oak for hull frames stood up well until the 1760s,
by the Napoleonic Wars the navy was scouring the world for timber of
all sorts. It even had teak warships built in India, though once again
it was Canada which proved its main salvation with ever larger supplies
of oak and pine.

In naval stores equally there were legislative attempts to secure
self-sufficiency. In 1689 England produced no canvas of its own and
the ensuing French war saw a great effort to build up an English sail-
making industry. An Act of 1696 offered a price preference of 2d a

yard for English sailcloth over comparable foreign products. Another
Act of the same year sought to encourage the growth of hemp and flax
and the manufacture of linen in England and Ireland as the raw material
for the industry. In 1713 there was an import duty on Dutch canvas
and a bounty for English exports. By the 1740s English sails were as
good and as plentiful as required both for naval and commercial needs.
Similar though less successful efforts were made to encourage colonial
production of hemp, pitch, tar, turpentine and resin to secure independence from Baltic suppliers. In 1704 a bounty was offered for their
production. It failed to produce any hemp for which Britain continued
to remain heavily dependent on Russia, but it did lead to £1,471,719
being paid out in bounties for pitch and tar, largely from the Carolinas,
between 1706-76. In practice however the dockyards still preferred
Swedish pitch and tar for quality and continued to purchase more from
Stockholm than North America, but this alternative source at least
induced the Swedes to keep down their prices to Britain and was a
ready stopgap in time of Swedish shortages.

Lastly there was the stimulus the navy provided for the metal
industries which proved fully equal to the demands made on them. It
was a major market for the iron industry in its demand both for cannon
and for fittings for ship construction, and in the 1770s the British navy
pioneered the large scale use of copper sheathing to protect ships'
bottoms from the ravages of the terredo navalis worm in tropical
waters, which greatly boosted copper production.

Although supply was a constant worry it never deteriorated into
a decisive weakness because in the last resort in the eighteenth century
the navy and the nation were determined to get ships at whatever the
cost. The cost could be enormous - the 100 gun 1st Rate Victory
cost £63,174 to build in 1765 and, including repair bills, £371,922 by
1815 - yet the Navy Board maintained a policy of always buying the best
materials - a policy that paid off. Overall Britain was much better at
keeping its ships at sea than its opponents.

4. Problems in creating a large Royal Navy: manpower

Having got its ships the government had then to man them. This
also involved two separate problems: that of creating a reliable
professional officer corps and that of securing a ready supply of seamen
to serve under them.

Officers

The heterogeneous collection of soldiers, adventurers, courtiers
and merchant officers who had hitherto officered the navy in wartime
were inadequate for the expanding navy with its new need for tactical
discipline and professionalism. It fell to Samuel Pepys as Secretary.

to the Admiralty to create with the backing of Charles II and James II
a disciplined body of professional naval officers. He sought to attract
members of the upper social classes into the corps since these had
the necessary aura of authority and habits of honour and personal
service to the Crown. They were lured in by the very close interest
of the royal brothers in the navy which made the service socially
respectable. Pepys equally sought to train the new officer intake to
seamanship at an early age and devised a means for them to break into
the old closed system of officer apprenticeship as captain's 'servants'
which depended on the patronage of and selection by serving captains.
The 'volunteer-per-order' was instituted, entering the service aged
13-16 and furnished with a king's letter ordering a captain to take him
on board for training. Rules were established for junior-officer
promotion requiring two years sea service for midshipmen and three
(including one as midshipman) for lieutenants, who additionally were
required to pass an examination in seamanship and be over the age of
20. Even then promotion was not automatic but depended upon appoint-
ment to a specific post by the Admiralty which gave priority in
appointments to the volunteers-per-order.

To provide professional continuity the Crown in 1667 began
retaining captains on half-pay when they were not in active employment.
This was a very limited measure at first applying only to captains of
1st and 2nd Rates in winter in wartime, but gradually it was extended.
In 1674 the same captains were granted half-pay until they found
employment in peace. In 1676 junior officers were allowed the chance
to stay in employment in a new lower rank of 'midshipman extraordinary'.
In 1693 Parliament both doubled the pay of serving officers and extended
half-pay to all captains, first lieutenants and masters demobilized at
peace. Reasons of economy led to a limitation on numbers in 1700 but
at the peace of 1713 half-pay was permanently extended to all captains
and lieutenants who might in future be required for active service and
to the senior thirty masters.

By 1718 the professional standard of this officer corps was such
that the Admiralty could decree that all promotion above captain should
be by strict seniority. By 1729 the social standard was such that the
volunteer-per-order could be abolished. It was replaced by a Naval
Academy at Portsmouth, but in practice this seldom attained its
establishment of forty cadets and the captain's servant system was
again allowed to predominate for sea-training (since the captains were
now generally socially acceptable and professionally competent their
judgement could be depended upon). In both the 1702-13 and 1739-48
wars naval expansion necessitated a considerable intake of merchant
officers (44% of all lieutenants commissioned between 1702-12), but
thereafter there was a sufficient stream of applicants from the landed
and wealthier professional classes for the corps to be considered
predominantly one of gentlemen. By the end of the century the percentage
of noble to non-noble officers in the navy was nearly double that in the

army. By the end of the century there was also a clear naval officer caste: nearly a quarter of the officers of the 1793-1815 wars whose biographies have been ascertained were sons of naval officers and presumably many more gained an entrée through family relationship to naval officers (Nelson was a clergyman's son but his maternal uncle was a naval captain who took him in as a captain's servant). [5]

The attractions of the naval officer corps by the second half of the eighteenth century were that it was not only a socially acceptable profession for the propertied classes but it was a successful profession with a strong esprit de corps. In 1749 officers were given an official uniform (their men had to wait another century). Their success-rate was far higher than that of the army and moreover the nation was prepared to honour its sailors for their successes. A notable triumph in a single ship-to-ship action could bring a captain a knighthood or baronetcy (it earned John Jervis a Knighthood of the Bath in 1782). Success in a major battle could earn the admiral responsible a peerage (Sir John Jervis was made Earl of St. Vincent in 1797). Far more sailors than soldiers broke into the ranks of the peerage and titled gentry in this way between 1689 and 1815. There was of course a corollary in that the nation was prepared equally to execrate more its unsuccessful admirals: the Earl of Torrington was imprisoned and disgraced in the 1690s for his defeat off Beachy Head; John Byng was executed in 1757 for failing to save Minorca.

Such exacting public standards may have intimidated the meek, but in practice most British naval officers developed an aggressive fighting spirit which distinguished them from all but a few of their opponents. This was helped by the fact that chances of professional and social promotion were backed by high financial rewards for success. The motivating force of prize-money in the war at sea was fully recognised by Crown and Parliament. In the seventeenth century the Crown and the Lord High Admiral claimed up to half the value of prizes but by the Cruisers and Convoys Act of 1708 Parliament gave it all to the captors - for 'the better and more effectual encouragement of the sea service'. The distribution of prize-money amongst the captors now established by proclamation did not materially alter the former system whereby a third went to the captain, a third to his officers, and a third to the crew, but because the captors now received the whole value of their prize this was a substantial inducement to enter the service and a substantial reward for aggressive conduct.

This was particularly true for officers since the lion's share of the spoils went their way (Table L).

Table L

Distribution of prize-money 1708-1808

$\frac{3}{8}$ captain (if serving under a flag-officer one of these eighths would be deducted for the latter)

$\frac{1}{8}$ equally divided amongst marine captains, sea-lieutenants and the master

$\frac{1}{8}$ ditto amongst marine lieutenants, boatswain, gunner, purser, carpenter, master's mate, surgeon, chaplain

$\frac{1}{8}$ ditto amongst midshipmen, carpenter's mate, boatswain's mates, gunner's mates, corporals, yeomen of the sheets, coxwain, quartermaster, quartermaster's mates, surgeon's mates, yeomen of the powder-room, marine sergeants

$\frac{2}{8}$ ditto amongst trumpeters, quarter-gunners, carpenter's crew, steward, cook, armourer, steward's mate, gunsmith, cooper, swabber, ordinary trumpeter, barber, able-seamen, ordinary seamen, volunteers by letter and marine soldiers

Source: English Historical Documents VIII p.834:
Proclamation regulating the distribution of prize and bounty money published in the London Gazette 27-31 May 1708.

In the 1739-48 war it was possible for a captain such as Rodney to gather prize-money to the extent of £15,000 between June 1744 and March 1748 when his pay and allowance cannot have totalled more than £1,100. Admirals, levying an eighth share of all prizes taken by ships under their command,were still more fortunate: Sir Hyde Parker was alleged to have made £200,000 as commander-in-chief of the Jamaica squadron between 1796-1800. The greatest source of inspiration for all future aspirants to the navy seems to have been the capture of the Spanish treasure ship Hermione by the Active and Favourite in 1762. The pay-out for this single lucky encounter was fabulous. The flag-officers' eighth went to Admiral Sir Charles Saunders (£43,309) and his commodore Sir Percy Brett (£21,654), neither of whom was present at the action. Captain Sawyer of the Active got £65,053 and Commander Pownall of the Favourite £64,873. Their lieutenants received £13,000 each.[6]

A prize such as the Hermione was unique. £50 here, £100 there were more likely to be the norm and even sums like this were not very frequent except for the lucky few cruisers. Nevertheless prize-money undoubtedly attracted officer-recruits into the navy and probably made officers greedy to the jeopardy of naval efficiency. Frigates would often chase prizes to the neglect of their normal escort and reconnaissance functions, and many of the ablest officers preferred to seek the chance of fortune in a frigate rather than chafe in a slow battleship in the line of battle. Augustus Hervey once unsuccessfully offered a captain of a smaller warship £400 to exchange for Hervey's 74 so as to get a better chance to go prize-catching. The Admiralty recognized the temptation to foresake enemy warships for more lucrative commercial targets and sought to provide alternative inducement. In the seventeenth century it paid £10 a gun for captured warships and increased this to £5 a man of their crews in the eighteenth century. This was still not comparable with good commercial prizes however and hence the use of promotions and honours to encourage warship actions.

There can be no doubt of the success of Pepys and his successors in establishing a large professional officer corps to service the navy, though the system was not without its failings. Excessive lust for prize-money was one, the use of 'Interest' to bend the rules and take short cuts to the rank of captain was another. Although the sea-service requirement for promotion to lieutenant was increased to 4 years in 1703 and to 6 in 1729, a boy with 'Interest' could get himself entered on the books of a ship commanded by an obliging relative, patron or client below the minimum age of 13, earn a paper sea-service without going to sea, and with this qualification and the falsification of his birth certificate attain a lieutenancy before the minimum age of 20. 'Interest' thereafter could ensure rapid selection from the ranks of lieutenants to the post of captain. Only then did 'Interest' run up against the seniority barrier, but early promotion to captain ensured a boy with 'Interest' a strong chance of promotion to admiral. Nelson was lieutenant at 18 and captain at 20 thanks to his 'Interest' with his uncle Captain Maurice Suckling, Comptroller of the Navy. The seniority system from captain upwards was a partial limitation on abuse but even this had a major drawback in that, with no official provision for retirement, the navy was top-heavy with aged admirals and captains blocking the promotion of able less senior men below them. To get an able captain or commodore a fleet command, all captains senior to him had to be promoted to admiral and then left without post on half-pay - an expensive price to get talent to the top.

Lastly, despite its _esprit de corps_ in the face of the enemy, the officer corps was often riven with feuds. Although the seventeenth-century jealousy between 'tarpaulins' and 'gentlemen' was overcome by the rising social status of officers in the eighteenth century, the service then took on the political feuds of the upper classes instead. The facility for serving officers to sit in Parliament not only embarrassed the Admiralty which could be publicly criticized by its officers on the floor of either House, but it also led to personal feuding. Naval feuds were fought out in Parliament, political feuds were fought out in the fleet. The eighteenth century abounds in resultant Courts-Martial. Two admirals and eleven captains were tried after one battle off Toulon in 1744, and the government Court Martial of the opposition admiral, Keppel, in 1778 led to the latter, along with two other opposition admirals, refusing to serve. This state of affairs has usually been thought to have been brought under control at last in 1806 when Lord Barham refused leave of absence for serving officers to attend Parliament, but this failed to stop Cochrane from opposing a Commons' vote of thanks to his admiral, Lord Gambier, for the destruction of the French fleet in the Aix Roads in 1809. It was more likely Cochrane's subsequent disgrace and the depoliticising of the navy in the long years of peace that followed which eased this sort of explosive tension.

There were limits to the efficiency of this officer corps therefore which might have torn it apart if it had been less successful. What kept it together was sucess in battle, in prize-money and honours which made it a going profession.

Seamen

Of all the problems in creating and maintaining the Navy, that of finding the seamen to man the ships proved to be the most critical.

The prime necessity was to create an ample reservoir of trained seamen which could be tapped by the navy. This was secured through the growth of maritime commerce backed by the 1651 and 1660 Navigation Acts which stipulated that the English ships, to which this expanding trade was to be confined, should be at least two-thirds manned by English seamen. The ability of the navy to protect most of this trade avoided the recourse to neutral ships to which the French were often reduced in wartime and which so paralysed French shipping and restricted the reservoir of trained French seamen to about 65,000 throughout the eighteenth century. At the end of the seventeenth century the number of English seamen were variously estimated at 50-80,000: nearly 5,000 in the North Sea colliers; probably the same in the distant fisheries (the Newfoundland fishery was reported as employing 8,000 men in 1740); 11-12,000 in the overseas trade; and about 30,000 in the coastal trade, exclusive of those already in the navy. At the end of the eighteenth century, in 1792, a Board of Trade report put the total number of seamen at 118,000.[7]

There was therefore an increasing number of seamen available. The problem then became one of inducing them to transfer to the navy when needed. When it wanted men the navy offered a bounty for volunteers. In 1739 this was 2 guineas for able-seamen and 30 shillings for ordinary seamen. In a crisis this could be stepped up, as in 1741 when it totalled £5 and £3 respectively, and loyal corporations might top up the bounty still further as a patriotic gesture: in 1793 Southampton offered an additional 3 guineas for able-seamen and $1\frac{1}{2}$ guineas for landsmen to its citizens to volunteer for the navy. In practice however it was not enough. Between 1738-48 the navy only paid 4,811 bounties to volunteers when from 1741 onwards the service required over 40,000 men.

Reasons for such lack of enthusiasm are not hard to find. A pay rise in 1653 took naval pay to 24 shillings a month for able-seamen and 19 for ordinary seamen. From this 6d was deducted for health insurance, 4d for the chaplain and 2d for the surgeon and in addition seamen had to buy their own clothing. Nevertheless free food and subsidized hospital care made pay in the seventeenth century comparable to the merchant seaman's 25 shillings a month in peacetime. However the 1653 pay rise was the last that naval seamen received until 1797 (officers' pay was doubled in 1693, a quarter of which increase was retained in the economies of 1700). In the meantime merchant pay rose. A Newcastle collierman might expect 30 shillings-£2 a month in peacetime and 50 shillings-£3 a month in wartime when there was danger of attacks by privateers and by naval press-gangs. Merchant marine wages rose to a peak of 70 shillings a month in the winter of 1757-8 during the Seven Years' War. Moreover not only was naval pay vastly inferior to this but it was also notoriously in arrears and usually paid in tickets which could only be cashed at the Pay Office in London or sold at enormous discount to private money-changers at the ports. It is a damning indictment of the system that it was considered a great improvement which might encourage more volunteers when Parliament enacted in 1728 that in future seamen should receive at least two months pay every six months and after eighteen months of sea-service they should within two months receive twelve months pay in cash on board ship. In practice however it was still possible for an admiral or captain to find ways to delay payment in order to discourage desertion. Not until 1795 did seamen gain the right to assign part of their pay directly to their wives and families.

Not only was pay bad and in arrears but conditions were appalling with negligible leave and morbidity and mortality rates on overcrowded warships far higher than for the army, the merchant marine or the equivalent civilian age-group on shore. Lastly discipline was extremely harsh. Floggings were more numerous, though less severe, than in the army, but above all the unofficial discipline was more extreme. Boatswain's mates were adept at 'startings' (blows with knotted ropes), and in particular the drill of the navy - operating the heavy guns and sailing the ship - involved much more manual labour than the infantryman faced and hence was much more punishing when endlessly repeated as a form of discipline.[8]

To set against such drawbacks the navy could offer a degree of welfare and prize-money. Welfare came initially from the Chatham Chest instituted in 1590, financed by the deductions from seamen's wages and which Christopher Lloyd has described as 'the first contributory medical insurance scheme in the country'.[9] The Chest provided

pensions for those disabled on naval service though in practice mal-
administration resulted in frequent arrears or non-payment. In the
1690s the sailor's 6d was diverted to support the new Royal Hospital
at Greenwich, to which merchant seamen were required to contribute
equally, and which became a naval equivalent of the French _Invalides_
providing a home for superannuated and impoverished seamen.[10]

It is doubtful however whether many seamen entered the navy
looking for a pension for a shattered limb or rescue from pauperdom
in old age. The most powerful incentive the navy had to offer seamen
was prize money. Yet returns for seamen were poor compared with
their officers. The biggest-ever haul, that of the _Hermoine_ earned
the seamen involved £485 each - the equivalent perhaps of ten years'
wartime wages in the merchant service. Generally however they were
lucky if they received £20 from a prize - a few shillings or £1-2 was a
more normal prize take. When it is remembered that prize-money
went mostly to the frigates and sloops whereas most seamen were
cooped up in the ships of the line and that there was better pay and
more chance of prize money in a privateer, it is not to be wondered at
that so few volunteered. It is probable that less than 8% of ships'
complements were able seamen who had volunteered from the merchant
service in the Napoleonic Wars.

Since so few trained seamen volunteered and since government
would not sufficiently improve pay and conditions to encourage more
volunteers, other methods were needed to man the ever expanding wartime navy. Shipping was embargoed at major ports in an effort to
force unemployed seamen to join the navy. In 1740 a 35 shillings a
month limit was imposed on merchant seamen's wages to restrict the
pay discrepancy between civilian and naval seamen. But these were
expedients tinkering around the problem and the major resort of the
navy was to impressment.

From immemorial usage and from statute law beginning in 1378
the Crown had the power to press seamen aged 18-60 (reduced to 55 in
1739) into its naval service. Until the 1690s the press may have been
just about tolerable since crews tended to be recruited for the six
months or so of the summer campaigning season and then discharged
when their ships were laid up over winter. But the 1689-97 war instituted the practice of maintaining most seamen in constant service
throughout the war, turning them over to other ships when their own
had to be laid up. At the same time the number of pressed men required
mounted with the navy's continued expansion (see Table N), and thereafter reports of resistance to impressment grew and pamphlets urging
alternatives increased. The civil authorities, under pressure from
local inhabitants, became distinctly uncooperative and at times opposition to impressment became bloody. In September 1740 there was a
running battle from the Downs past the Nore between three naval warships and the homeward-bound East India convoy which drove off with

gunfire all the navy's attempts to get press gangs on board them. On shore hostility is best exemplified by the 'Battle of Portland' of 1803 which left sixteen of a press gang wounded and four of the civilians who attacked them dead. The local coroner indicted the press gang's officers for wilful murder and they were forced to stand trial at the Assizes where they were eventually acquitted on a plea of self-defence.

The alternative most often proposed to the haphazard arbitrariness of impressment was the French Inscription Maritime by which the entire seafaring population were obliged to register their names and could be called upon for one year's naval service in three or four. A Voluntary Register was enacted in England in 1696 but the inducements offered were insufficient to attract enough able seamen to register themselves and the scheme was abandoned in 1711. Only a full compulsory system on the French model might have worked (though the French system broke down in wartime), but this reeked of French absolutism. Merchant shipowners objected to the degree of information about and control over the activities of their seamen that this would have afforded government. 'Free Britons', particularly the propertied classes who were not liable to impressment, preferred the randomness of the press to a sophisticated regulating bureaucracy.

The press continued and the Admiralty countered resistance by increasing its organisational efficiency. By 1793 private-contract press gangs hired on shore to supplement warship gangs were replaced by the navy's own professional Impress Service. Michael Lewis calculates that 50% of the sailing crew (perhaps 38.5% of the total complement) of warships were pressed men in the later stages of the Napoleonic War.

Nevertheless impressment went only part of the way towards solving the manning problem. Although the number of available seamen nearly doubled in the eighteenth century, the needs of the navy trebled. From 1650 to 1815 there were never enough seamen to fill the navy without jeopardising the merchant marine. In peacetime the two were compatible because naval requirements were wound down but war always caused several years of initial dislocation of the merchant marine and of slow mobilisation of the navy as it sought to build up its manpower without destroying the commerce which was its life support. Such a quandary occurred at the start of the 1793-1815 wars. In 1792 the navy was 17,000 strong and the merchant marine 118,000. To man the navy to perform all its tasks adequately in these wars was to require over 100,000 men (the peak was 143,000 in 1808-9). If the necessary 83,000 plus were taken at once from 118,000 merchant seamen, British commerce would have been devastated.

This aspect of the problem was met by a series of expedients. Every effort was made to attract men into the merchant service to replace those taken by the navy. Wages were increased. An Act of 1704 empowered magistrates to apprentice pauper boys into the merchant

service.   Another 1704 Act relaxed the Navigation Act to allow
merchantmen to take on three-quarters foreign crews in wartime.
The navy too was forced to spread its net beyond the seafaring
population to solve the manpower crisis.   An Act of 1704
repromulgated Tudor legislation turning 'rogues, vagabonds and
sturdy beggars' over to the fleet.   Debtors could choose between
the Marshalsea or the Navy.   The Lord Mayor of London could send
drunkards and petty offenders to the fleet.   These categories tended
also to fill the Quotas imposed on each county and seaport in 1795.
Amongst the Volunteers perhaps a third were landsmen.   Another
8% of the sailing crew were boys aged up to 17 - many enticed into the
navy by the various foundling societies, such as the Marine Society,
founded for the purpose in 1756 - who while considered as seamen
were at best only apprentices under training.   Some 12% more of the
sailing crews were foreigners as the navy, like the merchant marine,
looked outside of the country to complete its needs.   A few of these
were volunteers, but many more were pressed: in the earlier wars
Danes and Swedes in particular, and Americans in later wars,
virtually all of them trained seamen (Table M).[11]

Table M

The composition of warship complements about 1812

% of total

Sailing crew		Marines and soldiers
Trained seamen	Apprentices and landsmen	23% volunteers, some foreigners
8% British volunteers	6% boys	
1% Foreign volunteers	4% British volunteers	
35% Pressed Men	4% Pressed Men	
8% Pressed Foreigners	11% Non-press conscripts	
52%	25%	23%

Source: adapted from M. Lewis, The Navy of Britain pp. 317-8.
23% Marines and soldiers is a mean based on ibid p. 318
and Lewis, Social History of the Navy p. 120 of seamen and
marines demanded 1794, 1800, 1804

Lastly 20-25% of the navy's requirements were for marines to
act as guards, sharp-shooters, landing and boarding parties.   The
first Marine Regiment of Foot was created by Charles II in 1664 and
after 1755 they were embodied on a permanent footing instead of being
raised anew for each war as hitherto.   Surprisingly, although they
had the advantage of soldier's pay (30 shillings a week) and sailor's
prize money, their ranks were not always easily filled.   In 1794,

for example, 12,115 marines were estimated for but only 7,908 obtained. The marines recruited 'by beat of drum' like the army and the navy lacked the power to press marines as it could seamen, so such shortages had to be met by ordering army regiments on board ship as temporary marines. Even using this expedient however some curious anomalies occurred. In 1740, with sickness raging among the few marines at Portsmouth and the army already called upon to supply the West Indies and Channel fleets, all the government could give Anson as marines for his voyage around the world, were 500 Chelsea Pensioners. Not surprisingly half deserted before they reached Portsmouth and the rest died before they reached Cape Horn on the outward journey. During the Nile Campaign in 1798 Nelson recruited Austrian grenadiers at Naples. When it came to the pinch, the navy got its men where and when it could.

Sickness

Getting men into the navy was only the first part of this man-power problem because they had then to be kept there, and this involved combatting sickness and desertion. A return to the House of Commons in 1762 stated that of 184,899 enlistments hitherto during the Seven Years War, 1,512 were killed in action and 133,708 lost to the service by other causes, primarily sickness and desertion. While we do not know the relative proportions of losses between these two factors in the 1756-63 war we do know that for the subsequent American War of Independence of 175,990 enlistments from 1774 to 1780 1243 were killed in action, 18,545 died of disease and 42,069 deserted.

The prime killers were scurvy, typhus, yellow fever (primarily in the West Indies), malaria and dysentery. Their ravages were facilitated by conditions and sources of recruitment. With so many men packed into the damp, unventilated gun-decks of warships, many from the lowest state of society diseased before pressed into the navy, with poor food and cheap rum which was consumed in vast quantities and weakened resistance, the disease problem was inevitable.

Yet the naval authorities were slow to act on this problem, probably because it was only acute when the navy expanded in wartime, and until late in the eighteenth century they concentrated their efforts on cure rather than prevention. It was not until 1653, under the Commonwealth, that four Commissioners of Sick and Wounded were established to superintend such matters and not until after 1748 that this Board retained a permanent existence instead of being reconstituted for war only. Throughout, moreover, it was encumbered with the care of prisoners of war. Until the 1689-97 war the navy had no hospitals of its own. The sick were deposited in London hospitals or boarded out at the seaports. In 1689 a building was bought at Plymouth

for exclusive use as a naval hospital and a local surgeon hired to take
charge. This same war also saw physicians appointed to the fleet
and to operational naval bases and also hospital ships hired on a
regular basis to accompany the fleet for the first time. The
improvement was limited. The sick-care function of the Royal
Hospital at Greenwich was abandoned before its other function as a
home for naval pensioners opened in 1705, and the navy continued to
contract out care of most of its sick in wartime. This both facilitated
desertion and impeded recovery. In 1740 the Port-Admiral at
Portsmouth complained to the Admiralty of

> '...the deplorable condition our Sick Men are in at their
> quarters in Gosport, crowded twenty or thirty into a little
> Ale or Ginn house, and two or three in a bed of different
> diseases, without proper nurses or people to look after
> them,...in this miserable way, they dye very fast'.[12]

To avoid such failings in 1746 the Admiralty at last began work
on a 2000-bed hospital at Haslar, Gosport, which was finally completed
in 1762 and staffed by its own naval surgeons and sick-attendants.
Between 1757-60 a 1000-bed hospital was built at Plymouth and smaller
hospitals, also run by the navy itself, spread to naval bases throughout the empire.

Such developments may have improved the recovery rate,
though mortality remained extremely high, but they failed to stop
seamen falling sick and being disabled from active service. In 1779
28,592 seamen were recorded sick in the course of a year when
80,275 were borne on ships' books. The continuing high sickness
rate forced the navy belatedly into pioneering health reforms in the
second half of the eighteenth century. Greater efforts were made
at regular provisioning with fresh vegetables to avoid scurvy during
the 1756-63 war, and this at last made possible the close blockade of
the French ports by greatly prolonging the cruising power of the
Channel fleet. However it was not until the 1790s that independence
was secured from the victualling ships by adopting the naval surgeon
James Lind's recommendation in his Treatise on Scurvy of 1753 of
the use of orange and lemon juice. The results were sensational
both in enabling close blockade to be continued in bad weather when
fresh vegetables could not reach the fleet, and also (along with copper
sheathing of hulls) in strengthening the navy's power to make long
distance cruises overseas. Whereas Anson lost 1,051 of his 1,955
men in his 1741-44 voyage around the world, the Suffolk 74 could
voyage to India non-stop in 1794 without losing a man.

Other lesser reforms also accumulated into a major reduction
of the sickness problem. Admiral Vernon initiated the dilution of
rum into 'grog' in 1740. To reduce typhus the Admiralty in 1781, at

Lind's instigation, instituted receiving-ships where recruits were de-loused by scrubbing down and by having their old clothes replaced by Admiralty slop-clothing.   Sir Gilbert Blane, Commissioner for Sick and Wounded, besides being instrumental in the issue of citrus juice against scurvy, introduced scrubbing decks with 'holy-stones' rather than water to reduce dampness on board.   In the 1790s, Dr Thomas Trotter, Physician to the Channel Fleet, introduced first innoculation and then in 1798 vaccination against smallpox (the first time this preventive was used on a large scale).   These reforms reached a peak in the 1790s and enabled Blane to show that in consequence the number of seamen sent sick to hospital as a ratio of the number of seamen voted by Parliament fell from 1 in 2.4 in 1779 to 1 in 10.75 in 1813.   The total number of deaths as a ratio of numbers borne on warships also fell from 1 in 15.4 between 1776-80 to 1 in 29.58 between 1810-12.[13]   Such savings in manpower undoubtedly made possible the maintenance of such a large fleet and the success of the British close blockade of the Continent in the latter period.

Desertion

The greatest part of the navy's manpower losses came from desertion.   In view of the methods of naval recruitment and conditions in the service this is hardly surprising.   To prevent desertion the navy employed a variety of expedients.   Shore-leave could not be allowed and Captains sought to satisfy their frustrated seamen by allowing armadas of prostitutes to be ferried out to their ships when in port.   Pay was kept long in arrears on the old naval maxim of 'keep the pay, keep the men'.   Flogging was the inevitable penalty if a deserter was caught.   The fear of desertion indeed limited efficiency since it restricted shore-parties to trusted volunteers and hence impeded such necessary activities as loading or unloading stores, or watering.   Such restrictions have been blamed for the delays in the preparation of Sir Chaloner Ogle's squadron for the West Indies in 1740 for example.   By confining the men to the ship they were exposed more readily to the spread of disease, and by creating discontent was encouraged the very desertion which such precautions were designed to prevent.   Many officers saw the desirability of a more humanitarian treatment but despaired of its practicability while impressment was the mainstay of the fleet. If the sickness problem diminished, the desertion problem considerably increased during these wars.

Discipline

The final part of the manpower problem was that even if men were secured and sickness and desertion avoided, they had still to be turned into an effective, reliable fighting unit.   This was achieved by constant drill, backed by punishment for the laggardly, and both carried to an extent unknown in other navies.

Drill and punishment were supplemented by indoctrination. Charles Reece Pemberton, a volunteer of the Napoleonic Wars, reminisced that:

'...as often as he had seen days in the year, the English sailor had been told that he was "a true born Briton"...he was told that peer or peasant, his rights were the same: he was told that glorious independence and freedom from the scathe of tyranny were his inalienable heritage...[and]...that an unflinching spirit in resisting oppression, and driving back encroachment, and in insisting on and maintaining all these privileges and blessings, were the characteristics which distinguished a manly Englishman - a bold Briton, from all other men in the universe'.

Pemberton ironically contrasted the way in which this patriotism was drummed into the seamen to fight their foes with the way the message was ignored in the treatment imposed on and accepted by these same seamen from their own officers. There were many just, merciful and considerate officers whom the men would obey willingly, but Pemberton thought that:

'...half the ships in the fleet during the last war contained crews that required only a spark to start them into open mutiny; the combustion was daily accumulating under this toil from the caprice of officers and their vexatious niggling discipline'. [14]

The compulsory enlistment and conditions and treatment on board ship might well make a modern reader wonder not that the great naval mutinies of 1797 took place, but why they did not occur sooner. A number of factors might be adduced in explanation. Firstly although naval life was harsh, measured against the standards of its own time it was less harsh than it might seem today. At the very least the men had employment and an organised system of welfare to support them. Above all they were born into an hierarchical society and bred to accept authority, especially in a life at sea where the fate of their ship and their own lives might depend on the prompt execution of an order. Sailing a ship required operating as part of a team in which there was seldom place for individuality or independent thinking. Seamen were thus trained to obedience even before they entered the navy and the drill and punishment of naval discipline merely completed this mental attitude. Pemberton complained that his shipmates

'...were ship machinery...I never knew men whose speech
and action exhibited so little glimmering of intellectuality.
They had been trained into breathing automata'.[15]

This psychology of obedience was reinforced by the god-like
aura of authority which the navy built up about its Captains: the
elaborate ceremonial whenever they boarded their ship or came on
deck; the absolute powers bestowed on them in their office for all
but capital offences and which were increased by their isolation at
sea from any higher authority to which a sailor might appeal.
Captains and, through them, other officers, separated from the
men by the quarterdeck, usually by class and education, and by
wearing sword and uniform, were gods on a ship in face of whom a
seaman might well feel inferior. The system moreover was careful
not to make the distinction absolute for fear of total alienation. The
hierarchy of under-officers gave seamen the chance (remote though
it might be) to rise to the ranks of the gods and so encouraged them
to accept the system, while the actual physical disciplining of
recalcitrants was administered by these under-officers who had
risen from amongst the seamen and who could thus be used to divert
animus away from the officers.

The navy also took a number of practical precautions against
mutiny. Since fire and mutiny were always considered the two
greatest dangers to a ship, the official Regulations and Instructions
enjoined officers to ensure that all parts of the ship were visited at
half-hour intervals at night.[16] The marines, with higher pay and
quartered separately from the seamen, nearly a quarter of the crew
and the only part constantly armed, were a protection to officers
and deterrent to mutiny. The Admiralty attitude to mutiny was
consistently firm. Of necessity it was lenient to the majority of a
mutinous crew, but it usually insisted on making severe examples
of the ringleaders. For example, for mutiny on the Protée 64 in
1781 three men were flogged round the fleet at Portsmouth for 400,
500 and 600 lashes respectively and a fourth whose scheme it was
to seize the ship and take it over to the enemy was sentenced to be
hanged. The more serious the mutiny, the more zealously the navy
pursued and punished the mutineers. Mutineers from the frigate
Hermione who murdered their brutal Captain, Pigot, and most of
his officers and surrendered their ship to the Spanish in 1797 were
still being pursued and hanged by the navy in 1806.

Lastly, whilst there were always isolated mutinies on
individual ships (mostly over arrears in pay), most seamen probably
saw desertion as the main outlet for their grievances. However,
as with the French army, the long pent-up discontents finally came
to a head towards the end of the eighteenth century. The difference
was that, whereas the French army could capitalize on the Revolution

to voice its discontent, the British navy had no such domestic upheaval
to exploit and eventually the seamen organised their own mass protest.
It was a period when organisation to demand radical political reform
was beginning to be picked up by the masses from the propertied
classes. More particularly some naval officers blamed the Quota Acts
of 1795 which brought a more educated class of landsman into the navy,
men of some legal knowledge, prepared to organise and petition for
redress of grievances. In April 1797 the Channel Fleet mutinied at
Spithead, followed in May by the North Sea fleet at the Nore. The
demands of the Spithead mutineers were extremely moderate: improved
pay; better provisions; better care of the sick; more shore-leave; and
the removal of sadistic officers - and they promised to sail against the
French if the latter put to sea. Before their disciplined pressure a
grudging government and parliament gave way. Pay was increased by
5s 6d a month for ables and 4s 6d for ordinary seamen, and concessions
were made to all the other demands except that for shore-leave on
which the seamen themselves accepted the impossibility of all they
asked. The Nore fleet asked for more and held out longer, for a time
actually blockading the Thames, but the government refused to concede
more and their mutiny collapsed in June, enabling the Admiralty to
restore discipline by making examples. Whereas the Spithead mutineers
had been able to insist upon and obtain a full royal pardon, at the Nore
the Admiralty hanged 29, flogged 9 and imprisoned 29 more.

The great mutinies of 1797 constituted an important psychological
turning point for the navy which no-one forgot. Over the next two
decades the number of mutinies was more frequent as seamen saw
what organised protest could achieve, and slowly conditions improved.
In 1806 there was another pay rise. In 1808 the allocation of prize-
money was redistributed so that the captain lost one of his eighths to the
lower deck, the last two categories of Table L now receiving 4/8ths of
the total. Unofficial punishments were banned: running the gauntlet was
prohibited in 1806, and 'starting' in 1809 following a mutiny on the
frigate Nereide.[17] All this helped to maintain discipline.

5. Problems in creating a large Royal Navy: administration

Although there was a vast increase in the size of the navy and in
consequence of government intervention in the economy and in the lives
of its subjects, there was surprisingly little change in the basic shape
of naval administration to accommodate this growth. The main burden
of expansion was taken by the Navy Board, created in 1546 to administer
the financing and maintenance of Henry VIII's fleet, which now,
despite brief periods of economy, increased steadily in size. As
certain of its functions became too large for the Board they were hived-
off in ad hoc fashion to new subordinate bodies. Victualling went out
to contractors and after 1683 to a Victualling Office. The Treasurer
of the Navy moved out to his own Pay Office. The Sick and Wounded

Board appeared in wartime and permanently after 1748. A separate Transport Board emerged between 1689-1713 and from 1794.

Nevertheless this bureaucracy remained small. The Victualling Office, one of the two biggest purchasers of agricultural produce in the country, had a London staff in 1747 of 7 commissioners with 66 specialist officers and clerks and perhaps 60 more at eight victualling depots at naval bases. The Navy Board itself rapidly expanded its directing 'Principal Officers'and'Commissioners'from 4 to 10 in wartime after 1660 and from the Commonwealth onwards began to appoint resident commissioners to the naval dockyards to strengthen central control. Thereafter the number of commissioners remained at more or less the same level in the eighteenth century while their London office staff doubled from 63-67 in the mid-1690s to 116 in 1800. Yet not until 1796 was there a fundamental reorganisation and rationalisation of the Navy Office - on the report of Commissioners enquiring into the efficiency of all government departments - and only in 1832 was the most basic reform accomplished of amalgamating the Navy Board into the Admiralty Office.

The Admiralty Office was the one major emergent force of the era of expansion. Yet the development of a secretariat for the Lord Admiral's Office in the period 1660-88 seems less a planned response to the needs of expansion than the empire-building of an able bureaucrat, Samuel Pepys, who became Secretary to the Admiralty in 1673 and exploited the wish of Charles II and James II to retain a close personal control over the navy. The Lord Admiral had always exercised at least a nominal direction of naval affairs. Pepys now provided a professional secretariat, backed by royal authority, to enforce this direction. In addition to this and its former task of administering maritime law, Pepys also appropriated to the office the management of the personnel of the navy - hitherto unappropriated to any specific body but which had become a major administrative task now that the navy had become a permanent professional force and one of great size in wartime. Pepys gave the Lord Admiral (after 1688 put into commission of an Admiralty Board except for a brief period 1702-9) an Admiralty office to enforce its superiority over the Navy Board, though its bureaucracy was much smaller. In 1694 there were only two joint-secretaries and eight clerks at the Admiralty as against 51 clerks at the Navy Office and it was only in 1695 that the Admiralty acquired its own purpose-built offices. In the eighteenth century the Admiralty increased its control over the Navy Board by establishing port-admirals at naval bases who increasingly intervened in the activities of the Board's resident commissioners. This caused friction and near revolt between 1801-4 when the First Lord of the Admiralty, Earl St. Vincent,sought to purge the naval dockyards.

To add to this plethora of Boards and jurisdictions great and small the navy had no control over its own guns. These were supplied by the Board of Ordnance which had also to cater for the needs of the army. Finally, politicisation reached into the system in the eighteenth century as membership of these Boards became a tool of political patronage. The Navy Board alone largely managed to escape the political placemen and remained under professional seamen and dock-yard administrators. The seven-man Admiralty Board was redeemed by being chaired by an admiral or by a prominent politician nursed by an admiral on the board. Indeed the best that can be said for this ramshackle administrative 'system' was that it worked, and it worked better than it might have done thanks to the abilities in particular of four men: Pepys as Clerk of the Acts in the Navy Board 1660-73 and Secretary to the Admiralty 1673-9, 1684-9; Sir Richard Haddock, Comptroller of the Navy and head of the Navy Board 1682-1715; Admiral George Anson, later Lord Anson as a Commissioner and then First Lord of the Admiralty 1745-56, 1757-62; and Sir Charles Middleton, later Lord Barham, Comptroller of the Navy 1779-90, Commissioner 1794-5 and then First Lord of the Admiralty 1805-6.

7. Supremacy at sea: finance, aggression and national commitment.

In the last analysis Britannia came to rule the waves because the British navy was better financed than any of its rivals. Once disagreements with the Crown were overcome and a productive taxation and borrowing system established, Parliament never stinted on the navy because the whole country was convinced that national survival depended on it.

'To the question, what shall we do to be saved in this world ? there is no other answer but this, Look to your moat. The first article of an Englishman's creed must be, that he believeth in the sea...'

So wrote Lord Halifax in his Rough Draught of a New Model at Sea, published in 1694. No other European state possessed this utter conviction of the importance of maritime power to its very existence - not even Holland which increasingly diverted resources to its fortress barrier - and this was the crucial psychological difference both in financing and fighting the war at sea.

No continental Power possessed the resources to fight a war à l'outrance simultaneously on land and sea, and Britain always, usually successfully, sought continental allies to force its enemies to divert their main resources to their land frontiers, because being continental Powers their natural inclination was to strengthen their armies. In the wars between 1689 and 1713 France only spent 1/8th as much on its navy as on its army. In consequence between 1695-7 French naval shipbuilding slowed dramatically. In 1707 it stopped altogether. In contrast Britain spent 7/8ths as much on its navy as on its own and allied armies in these wars which became predominantly continental.

The classic case of this priority crisis for France came in 1760 when
with £7 million going to its army, it could only spare £$\frac{1}{2}$ million for
its navy and virtually abandoned the maritime and colonial struggle of
the Seven Years' War.[18]

Faced with this handicap, superior French naval administration
and better ship design were of no avail. Financial shortages had an
all-pervasive and disastrous affect on French strategy and tactics.
In the interests of conserving limited resources their fleet was usually
demobilized and only prepared for sea for specific expeditions. This
left the initiative to the British navy which kept at sea and gained an
enormous advantage in sea-training and practice at fleet-manoeuvres,
so that, whereas the better designed French ships were individually
faster than their British counterparts, British squadrons were
collectively faster because of better training. The French also sought
to avoid battle wherever possible because of the cost of repairs and
instead sought their strategic ends in other ways.

All this put the French, and Spanish also at a disadvantage when
actually forced to battle in the eighteenth century. It bred a defensive
and rather defeatist spirit which contrasted to the perpetual aggressive-
ness of a British navy convinced that only through seeking and winning
battles could the national trade and territory be ensured, eager for the
social and financial rewards of success, secure that battle damage would
be readily repaired at any cost in the naval dockyards, and in the course
of time brimming with the confidence of repeated success. It was in
these circumstances that the severe discipline and constant gun-drill of
the British navy paid off. Time and again eyewitnesses of fleet actions
recorded that the British ships maintained a heavier, more accurate,
and more sustained fire than their opponents. Together with the
expertise acquired at collective manoeuvring this gunnery superiority
enabled the British navy to develop the devastating tactic of breaking
through the enemy line in the late eighteenth century and ensure the
decisive victory which British admirals so often sought.[19]

From about 1693 onwards France indeed abandoned the attempt
to command the seas through fleet action and, since the Dutch also
cut back their battlefleet about the same time, no other continental
Power had the strength to do so. Whereas Britain maintained a fleet
of above 120 battleships, for much of the eighteenth century France
maintained only 60-70. The alternative was to raid British commerce
in a guerre de course but though this at times cut deep inroads into
British commerce, it never bit hard enough to bring Britain to its
knees and it had a corollary in that it left the maritime initiative to
Britain to attack France's coast and colonies and virtually bring French
overseas trade to a standstill. Only a battlefleet in control of the
Channel or off the Thames could have effectively stifled British
commerce,[20] but when towards the end of the eighteenth century the
French government sought to increase its battlefleet to bring the

command of the seas into serious contention once more, the financial effort contributed to the collapse of the Ancien Régime and to the French Revolution.

Ultimately the Bourbons paid the penalty for failing to realise, as British statesmen, merchants and gentry did, that naval command of the seas and mercantile wealth were inseparably connected. The one supported the other. By adopting the guerre de course France virtually abandoned its merchant marine for the duration of each war. In so doing it deprived itself of the trained seamen and commercial wealth necessary to sustain a very large navy and it fell so far behind in the naval arms race as to be unable to catch up without enormous financial and political repercussions. There was no short cut to supreme naval power. It had to be bought by heavy financial investment which did not shirk at the price. In the seventeenth and eighteenth centuries only Britain was prepared to make and sustain that sort of investment because only Britain was committed to a total belief in the importance and connection of trade and naval strength to the national welfare and because only Britain, as an island, had both the absolute need and the opportunity to make such a total commitment.

In making this investment Britain took a great step forward towards modern times. The build-up and maintenance of the Royal Navy were immensely important in shaping the development of the British state. They expanded the size of the British government, the extent of its intervention in the economy, and its interference with the lives of its subjects both for money and for manpower. Perhaps they made such extension of government power politically acceptable and paved the way for its further extension. The economic stimulus of building this navy, together with both the overseas sources of raw materials and tradeable commodities and also the overseas markets which it then won and kept, were substantial contributory factors towards the economic lead which Britain won over its continental counterparts in the eighteenth century, and which took it into industrialisation. The growth of the early modern British state was built on its seapower.

Table N

The Royal Navy 1578-1810

	Total ships	Ships of the line	Total tonnage	Men borne
1578	24			6,290
1603	42			8,346
1633	50			9,470
1660	156			19,551
1676	148	(58)[a]		30,260
1688	173[b]	100[b]		41,940
1702	224[c]	130[c]		38,874
1710	313			48,072
1715	224[d]	131[d]	167,596[d]	13,475
1727	233[d]	124[d]	170,862[d]	20,697
1741	228			43,329
1748	334	(126)[e]		44,861
1756	320			52,809
1762	432			84,797
1776	340			15,230
1783	617			107,446
1793	411[f]	113[f]	402,555[f]	69,868
1801	771[g]	127[g]	644,985[g]	129,340
1810	1,048[h]	124[h]	860,990[h]	142,098

Sources: figures are from Lloyd, The British Seamen, pp.31,80,286-9 unless otherwise stated.

a. This figure is for 1678 given by S. Pepys, Memoirs relating to the state of the Royal Navy of England for ten years, determined December 1688 (London, 1690) p.5. Pepys's figure may however only refer to battleships ready for sea.

b. Ehrman, Navy in the War of William III, p.4, which also gives the French navy as 221 ships including 93 of the line and the Dutch as 102 ships including 69 of the line.

c. Merriman, Queen Anne's Navy, p.363.

d. Baugh, Naval Administration 1715-1750, p.235.

e. Ibid., this figure is for 1749 when a report listed 291 total ships of 228,215 tons.

f.   James, Naval History, I, Table No.1. James gives the
     French navy in 1792 as 246 ships of which 86 were of the
     line (p.45). James's figures for total ships which Lloyd
     has followed includes harbour ships, ships building and
     ships ordered to be built. Of these 288 were available for
     sea service. The figure for ships of the line is of those
     actually available for sea service out of 153 total battleships.
g.   James, Naval History, III, Table No.9. Actual numbers
     available for sea service 511. Total battleships 190.
h.   James, Naval History, V, Appendix 18. Actual numbers
     available for sea service 729. Total battleships 243.

NOTES

1. The Navy in the War of William III, 1689-1697, (Cambridge, 1953)
   p.174.

2. D.A. Baugh,(ed.), Naval Administration, 1715-1750, (Navy Records
   Society, Vol.120, London, 1977) p.262.

3. See D.A. Baugh, British Naval Administration in the Age of
   Walpole, (Princeton, N.J., 1965) pp.323, 327-31.

4. Despite these disadvantages British dockyards seem to have been
   more efficient than the French if total workforce is a measure.
   J.R. Dull, (The French Navy and American Independence,
   Princeton 1975, p.256 n 29) gives the following figures for the
   French dockyard workforce in 1781: Brest 6,100-7,750; Rochefort
   2,725-4,160; Lorient 1,417-1,840; Toulon 3,280-3,860; Total
   14,522-17,610. Even allowing for expansion in wartime of up to
   a third of the 1772 figure, it seems likely that the French were
   employing a larger total workforce to maintain a navy nearly a
   third smaller.

5. Baugh, Age of Walpole, p.98; A.D. Harvey, Britain in the Early
   Nineteenth Century, (London, 1978) p.23; M. Lewis, A Social
   History of the Navy, 1793-1815, (London, 1960) p.36.

6. The only general survey of prize money is P.K. Kemp, Prize
   Money. A Survey of the History and Distribution of the Naval
   Prize Fund, (Aldershot 1946), though his account of the Hermione
   distribution does not seem so accurate as that of G. Carr Laughton
   in the V.C.H. Hampshire, Vol.5, p.391.

7. Ehrman, Navy in the War of William III, pp.110-11; R.D. Merriman,
   (ed.), Queen Anne's Navy, (Navy Records Society, Vol.103, London,
   1961) pp.170, 184-8; C. Lloyd, The British Seaman 1200-1860,
   (London, 1968) pp.285-6. N.B. These figures are exclusive of
   seamen in the Royal Navy and they might be compared with Lloyd's

citation of a 1582 survey claiming 17,157 mariners (op.cit. p.34) and M. Oppenheim's citation of a 1628 return of 13,372 seamen and fishermen(A History of the Administration of the Royal Navy 1509-1660, London, 1896, repr. 1961 p.244). For the number of French seamen I am indebted to Professor J. Meyer of Rennes University.

8. For an example of this see C.R. Pemberton, The Autobiography of Pel Verjuice, (London, 1968), pp.219-21.

9. British Seaman, p.47.

10. In practice the greater number of alternative sources of employment for seamen, the high pay of merchant mariners, and the availability of parish poor relief meant that the number of Greenwich pensioners never remotely approached the number of ex-soldiers in the French Invalides, only reaching 2,710 in 1814.

11. The figures in Table M may be compared with statistics given by Dull for the French navy in 1781-2 when it totalled just over 90,000 men of whom 40,733 were trained French seamen. France hired large numbers of foreign seamen, conscripted landsmen and soldiers into the navy, and recruited untrained volunteers. The essential difference to Britain is the extent to which French naval demands drained France's reservoir of trained native seamen. Only 15,780 were left for the merchant marine. (French Navy and American Independence, pp.144 n 3, 256 n 30).

12. Quoted in Baugh, Age of Walpole, p.181.

13. Sir Gilbert Blane, On the Comparative Health of the Navy, 1779, 1814, reprinted in Lloyd, Health of Seamen, pp.198-9. N.B. The fall in the rate of mortality cited by Blane (pp.198-9) and quoted by Lloyd (p.133) was for hospitals only. I have reached a rate for total mortality in the navy as a whole by setting the figures for total deaths in 1776-80 and 1810-12 given by Blane (pp.206,176) against the number of men borne on ships' books in these same years in Lloyd, British Seaman, pp.288-9.

14. Pemberton, Pel Verjuice, pp.147-8, 225.

15. Ibid., p.107.

16. For example see Regulations and Instructions relating to His Majesty's Service at Sea established by His Majesty in Council, (1808) p.174.

17. For the Protée ('Prothée') mutiny see A. Geddes, Portsmouth during the Great French Wars, (Portsmouth, 1970) p.5. See also J.D. Spinney, 'The Hermione Mutiny', The Mariner's Mirror, Vol.41 (1955) pp.123-36, and C. Lloyd, 'The Mutiny of the Nereide', Ibid., Vol.54 (1968) pp.245-51.

18. R. Pares, 'American versus Continental Warfare 1739-63', The

<u>English Historical Review</u>, Vol.51 (1936) pp.451-3: 120 million livres for the army as against 9 million for the navy. In this same year the British Parliament made appropriations of £4½ million for the navy, £8¼ million for the army, and £682,000 for the ordnance. In fact even when France had no continental distractions it still lacked the taxable capacity and credit-worthiness to match British naval expenditure. Dull has calculated cash appropriations for the French navy between 1776-1783 as in excess of £40,526,000, compared with British appropriations of £46,129,000. Since a proportion of French appropriations (at least £½ million annually) had to go on colonial expenditure the discrepancy between British and French expenditure was even greater. When the debt that the respective navies could contract beyond their cash resources is added, the discrepancy becomes greater still. By 31 December 1783 the French navy debt stood at £5,964,000 and the British at £14,722,000 - a difference of the equivalent of more than a year's total cash allocation. The British navy was able to persuade creditors to accept its 'Navy Bills' or 'Victualling Bills' which accounted for most of the debt in the knowledge that these bills would be backed by Parliament which usually assimilated them into the National Debt at the end of each war. See Dull, <u>French Navy and American Independence</u>, p.349; B.R. Mitchell and P. Deane, <u>Abstract of British Historical Statistics</u>, (Cambridge, 1971), pp.390-1; <u>House of Commons Journals</u>, Vol.39 p.957.

19. J. Cresswell, <u>British Admirals of the Eighteenth Century</u>, (London, 1972), pp.255-6 <u>et pasim.</u>

20. The Dutch achieved such a position in 1667 when Britain was saved by the Peace of Breda. The French achieved it in 1690 and 1779 but each time their stranglehold was broken by the outbreak of disease in their fleet.

BIBLIOGRAPHICAL NOTES

General Reading

The seminal work on the Military Revolution is that of Michael
Roberts 'The Military Revolution, 1560-1660', most easily available in
M. Roberts Essays in Swedish History, (London, 1967) pp.195-225.
This should be read in conjunction with the criticisms of Geoffrey
Parker, 'The "Military Revolution" - a myth?', Journal of Modern
History XLVIII (1976) pp.195-214. Parker sets the Revolution in the
context of longer-term European military development in his chapter
on 'Warfare' in The New Cambridge Modern History Vol. XIII
(Cambridge, 1979) pp.201-219, as does Michael Howard, War in
European History, (Oxford, 1976).

By far the best detailed survey of developments in military
organisation and their impact during the Military Revolution is that
by Fritz Redlich, The German Military Enterpriser and his Work Force.
A Study in European Economic and Social History, 2 vols. (Wiesbaden,
1964-5). A. Corvisier, Armées et sociétés en Europe de 1494 à 1789
(Paris, 1976) also provides a useful broad survey and is now in print
in translation (see p.87). More specialised accounts are cited in the
bibliographical notes to the individual articles below.

Plunder and the Rewards of Office in the Portuguese Empire

For English readers the best way to approach the study of the
Portuguese eastern empire is through the original sources published
by the Hakluyt Society. Of particular value for the topic discussed
here are the following: W. de Gray Birch (ed.), The Commentaries of
Afonso de Albuquerque, 4 vols., (London, 1875-84); A.C. Burnell &
P.A. Tiele (eds.), The Voyage of Jan Huyghen van Linschoten to the
East Indies, 2 vols., (London, 1884); A. Gray & H.C.P. Bell (eds.),
The Voyage of Francois Pyrard de Laval, 2 vols., (London, 1887-1890);
H.E.J. Stanley (ed.), The Three Voyages of Vasco da Gama, (London,
1869).

A narrative history based directly on the main chronicles is
provided by F.C. Danvers, The Portuguese in India, 2 vols., (London,
1894), Cass reprint 1966.

Modern works of a general nature include C.R. Boxer, The Portuguese Seaborne Empire, (New York, 1969) and Donald Lach, Asia in the Making of Europe, 2 vols. (Chicago, 1965). These deal with a wide variety of topics in a more or less detailed fashion and are invaluable as background. A more detailed economic study of the empire is V. Magalhaes Godinho, L'Economie de l'Empire Portugais au XVe. et XVIe. siècles, (Paris, 1969).

Among the monographs which have been written on the Portuguese empire in the sixteenth century, the following have particular relevance to the history of their military organisation. M.N. Pearson, Merchants and Rulers in Gujerat, (Los Angeles, 1977), contains an excellent account of how the trade monopoly worked. A.R. Disney, Twilight of the Pepper Empire, (Cam. Mass., 1978) and N. Steensgaard, Carracks, Caravans and Companies, (Lund, 1973) describe the decline of the Portuguese economic system. There are good studies in English of the Portuguese captaincies in China, Japan and East Africa. These include C.R. Boxer, Fidalgos in the Far East, (Los Angeles, 1948) and The Christian Century in Japan, (Los Angeles, 1951). For East Africa there are detailed narrative histories by E. Axelson, The Portuguese in South-East Africa 1488-1600, (Cape Town, 1973) and The Portuguese in South-East Africa 1600-1700, (Johannesburg, 1960). The detailed history of the Mozambique captaincy can be discovered in these volumes. The Mombasa captaincy is the subject of a stimulating essay by C.R. Boxer in Fort Jesus and the Portuguese in Mombasa, (London, 1960). Land holding in East Africa is dealt with in M. Newitt, Portuguese Settlement on the Zambesi, (London, 1973).

Finally all students of the Portuguese empire in Africa must ultimately turn to the two great collections of documents, G.M. Theal, Records of South Eastern Africa, 9 vols. (Cape Town, 1898-1903) reprinted by Struik, 1962, and Documents on the Portuguese in Mozambique and Central Africa, 8 vols. (Lisbon, 1962-79).

The Military Revolution and the Professionalisation of the French Army under the Ancien Régime

Because of the lack of detailed research in many of the relevant areas, there exists no comprehensive treatment of the position of the army within the French state in the last two centuries of the Ancien Régime. The best general introduction to the subject is A. Corvisier, Armies and Societies in Europe, 1494-1789, (English translation, Indiana, 1979), which contains material from his important doctoral thesis cited below.

The ablest introduction to the structure and functioning of the
absolutist state is P. Goubert, L'Ancien Régime. ii. Les pouvoirs,
(Paris, 1973). See also R. Mousnier, Les Institutions de la France
sous la monarchie absolue, 1598-1789, i, (Paris, 1974).

French military institutions in the early seventeenth century have
not received the serious attention of historians for many years. Sound
but obviously dated works are: G. d'Avenel, Richelieu et la monarchie
absolue, (4 vols., Paris, 1884-1890) (especially vol. iii); L. André,
Michel Le Tellier et l'organisation de l'armée monarchique, (Paris,
1906); and C. Rousset, Histoire de Louvois et de son administration
politique et militaire, 4 vols., (Paris, 1862-1863). To make up for
the shortcomings of these masterpieces of nineteenth century erudition,
more recent works on general administration in the early seventeenth
century may be consulted, in particular, R. Bonney, Political Change
in France under Richelieu and Mazarin: 1624-1661, (Oxford, 1978);
and D. Dessert, 'Finances et société au XVIIe. siècle: à propos de la
Chambre de Justice de 1661', Annales. Economies. Sociétés.
Civilisations, (1974). Particularly relevant for comparative purposes
in this key period are: F. Redlich, The German Military Enterpriser
and his Work Force. A Study in European Economic and Social History,
2 vols., (Wiesbaden, 1964-5); idem, De Praeda Militari. Looting and
Booty, 1500-1815, (Wiesbaden, 1956); and G. Parker, The Army of
Flanders and the Spanish Road, 1567-1659. The Logistics of Spanish
Victory and Defeat in the Low Countries' Wars, (Cambridge, 1972).

For military institutions in the late seventeenth and eighteenth
centuries, one work stands out: the superb doctoral thesis of A.
Corvisier, L'Armée française de la fin du XVIIe. siècle au ministère
de Choiseul. Le soldat, 2 vols., (Paris, 1964). Still useful for the
eighteenth century are E.G. Léonard, L'Armée et ses problèmes au
XVIIIe. siècle, (Paris, 1958); and A. Babeau, La Vie militaire sous
l'Ancien Régime, 2 vols., (Paris, 1889-1890).

For the lot of the common soldier, there is much to be gleaned
from the four volumes of the Encyclopédie méthodique, (Paris, 1784-
1797), devoted to 'Art militaire'. J. Colombier, Medecine militaire,
(Paris, 1778), is particularly useful for sanitary conditions. C. Jones's
article, 'The welfare of the French foot-soldier from Richelieu to
Napoleon', History, forthcoming, reviews the field of welfare provision
against the background of the general evolution of military institutions.

For the state of the army on the eve of the Revolution, the
essential work is now S.F. Scott, The Response of the Royal Army to
the French Revolution: the role and development of the Line Army,
1787-1793, (Oxford, 1978). D. Bien, 'La Réaction aristocratique
avant 1789: l'exemple de l'armée', Annales E.S.C., (1974), which
repeats and to a certain extent elaborates on points made in the work
of E.G. Léonard, cited above, is also useful.

The Foundations of British Naval Power

The best general survey of the Royal Navy is still Michael Lewis The Navy of Britain, (London, 1948). Five detailed accounts are absolutely essential for the study of the rise of the Royal Navy: M. Oppenheim, A History of the Administration of the Royal Navy and of Merchant Shipping in relation to the Navy, from 1509 to 1660, (London, 1896, repr. 1961); John Ehrman, The Navy in the War of William III 1689-1697, (Cambridge, 1953); R.D. Merriman (ed.), Queen Anne's Navy (Navy Records Society, Vol. 103, London, 1961); Daniel A. Baugh (ed.), Naval Administration 1715-1750 (Navy Records Society, Vol. 120, London, 1977); Daniel A. Baugh, British Naval Administration in the Age of Walpole, (Princeton, N.J., 1965).

In addition to these basic sources, private armament and the build-up of naval shipbuilding and dockyards can be studied in R. Davis, The Rise of the English Shipping Industry in the Seventeenth and Eighteenth Centuries, (London, 1962); R. Davis, English Merchant Shipping and Anglo-Dutch Rivalry in the 17th Century, (London, 1975); E. Keble Chatterton, The Old East Indiamen, (London, 1933); K.G. Davis, The Royal African Company, (London, 1957); The Victoria County History of Kent Vol. 2: 'Maritime History, The Royal Dockyards' by M.M. Oppenheim; The V.C.H. of Hampshire Vol. 5: 'Maritime History' by L.G. Carr Laughton; D.C. Coleman, 'Naval Dockyards Under the Later Stuarts', Economic History Review Vol. VI (1953-4); M.M. Oppenheim, The Maritime History of Devon, (Exeter, 1968); Alistair Geddes, Portsmouth During the Great French Wars 1770-1800, (Portsmouth Papers, No.9, 1970). The problem of material is dealt with, as regards timber, in R.G. Albion's Forests and Sea Power: The Timber Problem of the Royal Navy, 1652-1862, (Cambridge, Mass., 1926) summarized in The Mariner's Mirror Vol.38 (1952). Other naval stores are covered by J.J. Malone in 'England and the Baltic Naval Stores Trade in the Seventeenth and Eighteenth Centuries', The Mariner's Mirror Vol.58, (1972). See also, B. Pool, Navy Board Contracts 1660-1832, (London, 1966).

As regards manpower the basic sources above should be supplemented for the officer corps by M. Lewis, England's Sea Officers, (London, 1939). D. Erskine (ed.), Augustus Hervey's Journal, (London, 1953) and D. Spinney, Rodney, (London, 1969) provide excellent accounts of the lives of two successful naval officers of the eighteenth century. For the seamen Christopher Lloyd's The British Seaman 1200-1860, (London, 1968) is indispensable. C.R. Pemberton, The Autobiography of Pel-Verjuice, (London, 1929) provides a vivid account of a seaman's life in the Napoleonic Wars. For both officers and men M. Lewis, A Social History of the Navy 1793-1815, (London, 1960) is a classic study. The problem of disease is comprehensively dealt with in C. Lloyd and J.L.S. Coulter, Medicine and the Navy 1714-1815,

(London, 1961) and C. Lloyd (ed.), The Health of Seamen (Navy Records Society Vol. CVII, 1965). For the naval mutinies see G.E. Manwaring and B. Dobrée The Floating Republic, An Account of the Mutiny at Spithead and the Nore in 1797, (London, 1935 repr. 1966).

The growth of British Naval Administration is covered in the introductions to J.C. Sainty, Admiralty Officials 1660-1870, (London, 1975); J.M. Collinge, Navy Board Officials 1660-1832, (London, 1978) and in the basic books cited in the first paragraph of this bibliography.

The tactical problems of naval warfare are amply surveyed in J. Cresswell, British Admirals of the Eighteenth Century, (London, 1972).

Among monographs enabling a comparison with Britain's closest rival France, two in particular stand out: P.W. Bamford, Forests and French Sea Power 1660-1789, (Toronto, 1956) and J.R. Dull, The French Navy and American Independence, (Princeton, 1975).

Since the first Impression of this book the publication of Stephen Gradish's The manning of the British Navy during the Seven Years' War, (London, 1980) has clarified many aspects of that vital issue in one of Britain's most important wars, while the overall comparative aspects of the Anglo-French naval wars have been excellently portrayed by J. Meyer and J. Bromley, 'The Second Hundred Years' War (1689-1815)', in D. Johnson, F. Bédarida, F. Crouzet (eds.), Britain and France. Ten Centuries, (London, 1980).

Dr Michael Duffy is lecturer in History at the University of Exeter. Author of an article on the British expedition against Dunkirk in 1793 (English Historical Review, 1976), he is preparing a book on the British expeditions to the West Indies during the War against Revolutionary France.

Dr Malyn Newitt is senior lecturer in History at the University of Exeter. Author of Portuguese Settlement on the Zambesi (Longman, 1973) and several articles on the Portuguese Empire.

Dr Colin Jones is lecturer in History at the University of Exeter. Author of several articles on French social history in the seventeenth and eighteenth centuries, including 'The Welfare of the French foot soldier from Richelieu to Napoleon', History, 1980.

The cover illustration is based on an engraving by Guillaume de la Haye after Hubert Gravelot's Plusieurs positions dans lesquelles doivent se trouver les soldats, 1766.